I WRITE WHAT I THINK AND EVERYONE ELSE BE DAMNED

Beyond The Vale Publishing
www.beyondthevalepublishing.com

I WRITE WHAT I THINK AND EVERYONE ELSE BE DAMNED

By

Mugabe Ratshikuni

I dedicate this book to my late parents, Funzani Azwianewi Ratshikuni and Julie Nobakhe Ratshikuni. The sky is no limit because we truly stand on the shoulders of giants as your children and even your grandchildren. The ceiling of one generation is truly the foundation and stepping stone of the next generation, may your posterity be worthy of your outstanding legacy as trailblazers and pioneers.

Of course, the title of this book is inspired by the title of a well-known book by Bantu Steve Biko, with my own unique twist and flavour added to the mix. Having said that, I have no hubristic claims that this book will have the same impact as that timeless Biko text, but I do claim some inspiration from it when it comes to the title specifically.

I have a mate from varsity, Mahlatsi Movundlela, who often comments when I post my reputedly controversial and provocative articles and views on contemporary issues on social media and one of the phrases he likes using is, "Mugs, just like Biko, you clearly write what you like and fear no one." Unbeknown to him, the seeds of a book title were sown in that oft-repeated response of his to my social media posts and articles as well as opinion pieces.

I am a firm believer in the Socratic method of knowledge acquisition as well as dialogue and engagement, as I believe it fosters critical reasoning and produces more nuanced analysis within the "Public Square" as they would have termed it in the era of classical antiquity. I hope this comes across as you make your way through the various articles that make up the chapters of this book, because this book is really about searching for answers, a quest for better solutions to the human condition and the problems of society, it is an intellectual odyssey informed by the lamentations of young Africa.

The aim of the book is to steer us towards asking ourselves and those around us better questions in the pursuit of a better world, with the understanding that, "you can tell the intellect of any person, not by the responses they give, but rather by the questions they ask", as a mentor of mine when I was in my twenties was wont to say. I hope you enjoy the probing, pondering and reflective style of this book. In the words of the renowned American author William Faulkner, "the problems of the human heart in conflict with itself... alone can make good writing because only that is worth writing about, worth the agony and the sweat."

Mugabe Funzani Ratshikuni

Contents

Foreword

When American literacy expert and author Pam Allyn remarked that "Reading is like breathing in, and writing is like breathing out," she might not have had Mugabe Ratshikuni's I WRITE WHAT I THINK AND EVERYONE ELSE BE DAMNED in mind, but you get a sense that Ratshikuni is indeed exhaling through the pages of this book. After all, was it not our acclaimed novelist, poet, and playwright Zakes Mda who reminded us of the basics of reading and writing? "A reading culture," he said in 2017, "once cultivated produces more readers and more readers produce more writers."

It is the culture of reading, I believe, that has gifted us the deep philosophical, political, and provocative words that permeate this book. In the end, many will agree that Paul Sweeney was right when he said, "You know you've read a good book when you turn the last page and feel a little as if you have lost a friend." This is when you know you have interacted with a good text.

Indeed, I WRITE WHAT I THINK AND EVERYONE ELSE BE DAMNED is a timely intervention, as reflected in the first two sections of the first chapter, which discuss daily life experiences and the intersection of rugby, politics, and society. This alone is worth the read and crucial to get us talking. I am reminded of the euphoria and the cacophony that followed the Springboks' historic triumph in securing the fourth Webb Ellis trophy. Numerous articles and countless social media posts were written on how this remarkable achievement fostered national unity.

As he did in 2019 when he hoisted the trophy aloft, Captain Fantastic Siya Kolisi lived up to expectations by talking about unity with his "stronger together" mantra. It is this mantra that catapulted Kolisi to a cult figure in a rugby-mad nation, in the process elevating him to a latter-day Madiba, a saint of some sort. This mantra has left many spellbound, galvanising the country around a misleading notion of national unity. Many astute leaders from the corporate world to politics repeated the mantra ad-nauseam.

However, beyond the euphoria and commendation lies a narrative less explored. Beneath the surface of unity, a critical examination reveals complexities that extend beyond the realm of sports glory, prompting reflection on the broader societal implications of such a momentous win. This is what Ratshikuni does well.

His thought-provoking interventions compel us to reflect deeply on post-apartheid South Africa, a country for which many people were prepared to lay down their lives, but which still has far too many unresolved problems and unfulfilled promises, despite significant progress in certain areas.

The reflection on Cheeky Watson, a figure from what many White compatriots regard as a "controversial" family, forces us to engage with the uncomfortable question of transformation in sports and politics. The topic, in the words of Cheeky's son and former Springbok player, Luke, is enough to make one want to "puke" on the Springbok jersey.

Unfortunately, we cannot escape our reality, and the false notion of unity perpetuated amidst the rugby euphoria occurred in the context of the world's most unequal society. Thirty years since our democratic breakthrough, the sprawling shacks of Alexandra township still exist side by side with the palatial mansions of Sandton.

Recent data estimated South Africa's Gini coefficient to be around 0.67. This statistical measure, widely used for income distribution, shows that the closer the number is to one, the higher the inequality. Apart from being the world rugby champions, this is another of South Africa's long-held, undisputed global titles of shame: almost perfect inequality.

Another aspect of a good book is its subtlety in addressing complex issues. Among the key aspects of Ratshikuni's intervention is its intersection with deep ideological issues. For example, in "Death and the NHI", Ratshikuni helps us navigate the complexities of the National Health Insurance in its endeavour to achieve universal health coverage. NHI is not just another national discourse but rather an issue that can be understood in the day-to-day practical stories of ordinary South Africans and their class location. In this way, a detailed and lasting record of how the country navigates such historical events is captured.

Ratshikuni's approach is thought-provoking. In "Adam Smith, Capitalism and Morality", he scrutinises the discourse on nationalisation through a nuanced lens. The debate on nationalisation, especially the call for nationalisation of mines in 2011, led by the ANC Youth League, captivated post-apartheid South Africa, sparking divisive debates across class and racial lines. Another discourse that evoked intense emotions was the debate on land expropriation without compensation. It is ironic how neoliberalism has consistently prevailed in such discussions. But I digress.

The nationalisation debate thrust Julius Malema and the ANC Youth League into national and international political prominence, albeit making them adversaries in business circles. Advocates of nationalisation argued that it was a response to South Africa's socio-economic challenges.

However, Ratshikuni delves much deeper, invoking Adam Smith's Theory of Moral Sentiments, posing profound philosophical questions. Few, including myself, can fully engage at this level, leaving us with more questions than answers. Does Smith's emphasis on sympathy and moral judgments for social harmony obscure the underlying class conflicts within capitalist societies such as ours? While Smith's framework suggests that personal virtues and market interactions can achieve moral and economic equilibrium, did he adequately address the exploitative relations of production that fuel inequality and alienation? Can moral sentiments transcend the material conditions and social relations that shape our consciousness? Critics argue Smith's theory perpetuates and justifies the capitalist system, masking the realities of class struggle and the imperative for revolutionary change.

Ratshikuni challenges us to broaden our perspective if we are to resolve the myriad intractable problems facing our society.

Enter Julius Malema. Another controversial figure that Ratshikuni examines in his gaze into our society. Malema and his politics make us think about the concept of freedom and democracy. Can we really imagine "A World Without Politicians"?

We must really congratulate, or perhaps, thank Ratshikuni for this decisive intervention. Who would be brave enough to write about what Jimmy Manyi said about the replacing of White elites with Black elites? At a deeper level, these reflections remind us of Frantz Fanon's "The Pitfalls of National Consciousness" in his opus magnum The Wretched of the Earth. Fanon critiques the post-colonial elite for their failure to achieve true liberation, arguing that they merely replace colonial rulers while maintaining exploitative structures, resulting in continued oppression and economic stagnation. He emphasises the need for genuine, people-centred national consciousness and economic independence to avoid the pitfalls of neo-colonialism and achieve meaningful social transformation.

Indeed, the national question in South Africa remains unresolved and far from obsolete in the post-apartheid era. The neglect of this issue has exacerbated racial and ethnic tensions and xenophobia. Thandika Mkandawire, the late Malawian public intellectual, previously observed that discussions on the national question have been overshadowed by discourses on transnationalism, diversity, diasporas, marginality, and even 'rainbows'. Nonetheless, Ratshikuni's intervention serves as a stark reminder of the ongoing relevance of this complex issue of national unity and sovereignty, intertwined with inquiries into class dynamics. This prompts reflection on the role of the Black working class and their inclusion in decision-making processes. Scholars such as Mzala Nxumalo and Neville Alexander argue that this segment of society not only suffered national oppression but also faces exploitation as a class. Addressing this dual oppression remains a critical challenge.

This is what Ratshikuni's timely book forces us to ponder. In a relaxed way, we think about serious and deep questions that compel us to consider options for the future. But do not get too cosy because you will soon be onto "Wikileaks and American Hypocrisy". Another topic that makes one's blood boil.

I wrote somewhere that Julian Assange's plight exemplifies the complex interplay between power, justice, and media influence in our modern world. Assange was unfairly, if not illegally, incarcerated for well over a decade for his commitment to truth. In many ways, he embodies the spirit of Mandela for our time. Ratshikuni's critique of hypocrisy extends beyond the US to global society's silence on Assange's plight. The Western media, including those in South Africa, remained notably silent despite Assange's deteriorating health during his unlawful incarceration.

In stark contrast, the tragic death of Alexei Navalny, a Russian opposition leader, lawyer, anti-corruption activist, and political prisoner, in prison sparked widespread media attention and condemnation, particularly in the West. Western leaders and media outlets swiftly highlighted the injustice, praised Navalny's bravery, condemned his death, and put the blame squarely on Vladimir Putin's regime. Domestically, political parties like the DA and various media echoed these sentiments, offering "heartfelt condolences" in alignment with the Western narrative, while implicating the ANC by association with Russia.

Amidst this orchestrated outcry, Assange's case was met with a pervasive silence, despite his symbolisation of courage in seeking truth and transparency in the context of state repression and media manipulation. The recent release of Assange provides a glimmer of hope amid these circumstances.

But it is here where you realise that you are about to lose a companion. Separation anxiety sets in. But you will be glad for this companionship; it will be time well spent.

Congratulations, Mugabe Ratshikuni, for this masterpiece. Even if I am the only person who says so. Otherwise, I would be cooking the rice outside the pot.

Anyway, who cares!?

Prof Mandla J. Radebe

Author and Associate Professor: School of Communication
Director: Centre for Data and Digital Communication
University of Johannesburg
8 July 2024

1

Wannabe Philosopher

The Myth Of Equality

I remember attending a talk on transformation (or lack thereof) in SA rugby, given by Dan "Cheeky" Watson a few years ago, at a UCT lecture hall. As is his wont "Cheeky" as he is popularly known proceeded to make a few statements that the mainstream media would categorise as extremely controversial. The main thrust of Cheeky's talk was that there were enough good black rugby players in South Africa to ensure a greater representation in the Springbok team if the selection criteria were indeed merit-based, but that South African rugby had not done enough to ensure that this was indeed the case. Whether you agree with these sentiments or not, what struck me at that point and has stayed with me over the years was a question that was asked by someone during the Q&A session at the end of Cheeky's talk.

The question that was asked to Cheeky Watson was along these lines, "Cheeky, whilst I agree with your sentiments about the need for greater transformation in SA rugby and that more can indeed be done to ensure that there are more black players in the Springbok team, the question I have is: how are we going to counter the fact that the Afrikaans woman seems to have this inherent ability to produce human specimens like Pierre Spies, Bakkies Botha, Danie Rossouw etc who seem to be tailor-made to play the game of rugby, whereas black mothers seem to produce human specimens who don't necessarily have the size required to play the game?"

This question got me thinking again about an issue that has always seemed to bother me and which I periodically revisit intending to try to solve a few unanswered questions. The issue I am talking about is the issue of equality. The classical Greek philosopher, Plato stated that "all men are by nature equal, made all of the same earth by one Workman; and however we deceive ourselves, as dear unto God is the poor peasant as the mighty prince." Modern society has been built on the fundamental assumption that human beings are inherently equal and a lot of our expectations and perspectives on what is a just and fair outcome in society have been framed by this belief in the equality of all humans. Even the concept of democracy itself was borne out of the notion that all humans are equal as stated by the Greek philosopher Aristotle, "democracy arises out of the notion that those who are equal in any respect are equal in all respects; because men are equally free, they claim to be absolutely equal."

It is this belief in the equality of all humans that has led to all sorts of revolutions throughout history, chief of which was the French Revolution built on the promotion of the values of, "liberty, fraternity, and equality." This belief in the equality of all human beings becomes problematic when you take a glance around the world and see the inequalities that pervade society. It becomes difficult to justify the inherent equality of all human beings when all the evidence around us seems to point to high levels of inequality inherent in humanity. The socialists would have us believe that this inequality is a result of flawed social organisation which can only be solved by establishing a socialist order whereas the capitalists would have us believe that this inequality is not necessarily a problem, as long as we can create "equal" opportunity for all to flourish through the exercise of initiative, enterprise, and personal ingenuity.

The problem may just be our understanding of the concept of equality. Human beings are indeed equal as regards value, worth, and dignity. We all hold equal value, worth, and dignity irrespective of our social status or our position in life. However, it is also true that human beings are born inherently unequal when it comes to ability, talent, temperament, intellect, physical attributes, etc and that these differences play a major role in defining what we can or cannot accomplish in life. Maybe we have confused equality of worth and value with equality of ability and because of that, we find ourselves trying to engineer all sorts of social outcomes which go against the very nature of what we are as human beings. Going back to my rugby example, maybe we in South Africa are trying to counter natural forces by insisting that there be more black players in our rugby teams when the reality is that black South Africans don't have the physique and the natural attributes that are necessary to excel in the modern rugby game? With a few exceptions here and there the modern rugby game seems to be suited to big, strong, muscular individuals and in the South African context there are not many black people who possess these attributes when compared to their Afrikaner counterparts who seem to excel in the sport. Perhaps we should change our expectations when it comes to the number of black people that we expect to be in the Springbok rugby team. Maybe we are trying to enforce equality where nature prescribes inequality.

I use a rugby example in the South African context, but this logic can be applied to all kinds of socio-economic contexts where unequal outcomes have produced all kinds of revolutions, policies and resolutions aimed at reversing this inequality. It was the English author George Orwell who said that "no advance in wealth, no softening of manners, no reform or revolution has ever brought human equality a millimetre nearer." Maybe our worst mistake has been to mistake equal individual opportunity for equal group results. Perhaps we should all accept an unequal world when it comes to socio-economic outcomes because the reality of human inequality when it comes to talent and ability almost guarantees that there will be differing outcomes and results based on individual human effort and application. Maybe the socialist ideal, "none should have more than they need, whilst any have less than they need" as promoted in Robert Tressell's epic novel, The Ragged Trousered Philanthropists, is entirely unrealistic given the inherent inequality in terms of ability amongst human beings.

Proponents of "social justice" are always railing against the great gulf between the haves and the have-nots in society but what if all of this is the natural outcome of inherent human inequality? It was Aristotle who said that "the worst form of inequality is to try to make unequal things equal." Maybe we are guilty of trying to impose equality on inherently unequal beings. It would be difficult to argue against the fact that human beings are born with inherently unequal abilities and talent ceteris paribus. In other words, if you take away the differences in social status, financial muscle and access to resources and opportunities that human beings are born into, there are inherent differences in human beings which would produce unequal outcomes in any case.

These are the kinds of questions that I have asked myself over the years as I have reflected on the issue of equality and the supposed problem of inequality in the world. Looking at the South African context, where we live in one of the most "unequal" societies in the world, maybe we have made the mistake of shifting our emphasis from equality of prospective opportunity towards statistical parity of retrospective results and hence our battle with the implementation of policies such as Black Economic Empowerment, Affirmative Action, and all kinds of quotas in different sectors of society. To paraphrase a famous Orwellian phrase, maybe "all men are indeed created equal, but some are more equal than others."

The Concept Of Freedom

As I was watching the ANC's January 8 statement where it celebrated its 99th birthday, ANCYL leader Julius Malema said something in his short, fiery speech that got me thinking about the concept of freedom and what it means or should mean for us. Malema said the following, "President Zuma, we have a special request: lead us into economic freedom. You can vote until you are pink; as long as you don't have economic power, your vote is meaningless."

Naturally, these words evoked a strong response from the crowd that was gathered to celebrate the ANCs 99th birthday, but for me these words, whilst true from a factual perspective, are bothersome, because of the message that they send to South Africans about the notion of freedom and how it can be attained. The words uttered by Malema and cheered by large sections of the crowd at the ANCs birthday celebration shindig betray a certain, dangerous paradigm that we seem to have embraced as South Africans which in my view prevents us from becoming the winning nation that we aspire to be. This is the mindset or attitude that says that we can only be free if someone external to us takes us towards that freedom. In other words, our freedom as individuals is dependent on some kind of external political figure or messiah who will ascend to the throne and provide the solutions to all our problems. Can a society that is continuously looking for external messiahs be said to be truly free? To me, this sounds more like the attitude of slaves than of freemen. As stated by the American poet Ezra Pound, "A slave is one who waits for someone to come and free him." Africa's problems can be summed up in this one statement: our people are not truly free because they are still waiting around for someone to come free them when they are for all intents and purposes free to take charge of their own lives and destinies. This has led to an over-reliance on political messiahs and messianic political organisations, which has destroyed the continent and is at present killing the great potential that South Africa possesses.

What, in essence, is true freedom?

According to the French Existentialist philosopher Jean-Paul Sartre, "freedom is what you do with what's been done to you." This is an insufficient definition of freedom because it limits the exercise of freedom to a reactive rather than a proactive stance. Black Consciousness Movement leader Steve Biko argued that "freedom is the ability to define oneself with one's possibilities held back not by the power of other people over one but only by one's relationship to God and natural surroundings." Charles de

Montesquieu defined freedom as, "the right to do what the law permits." Biko and de Montesquieu's definitions of freedom provide us with some important qualities or attributes that should be characteristic of a truly free society. A society of free people is a society of individuals who are empowered to take charge of their destiny without being limited by the power of other people over them i.e. not reliant or dependent on politicians or any other external group of people but self-reliant, self-defined, and self-driven, with the only limitation being their relationship to God (or some Higher Power if you like) and to their environment (which consists of nature and other people around them). Secondly, a society of free people has a high regard for the rule of law and operates within its parameters. It is on these points that Africa and Africans are often found wanting and hence are not truly free. In the words of the German philosopher Hegel, "the history of the world is none other than the progress of the consciousness of freedom." It is only when we are consciously free, that we can actually develop and progress. Progress and development are linked to our consciousness of our freedom. If we are not aware of the fact that we are free, we will continue to pin our hopes on political messiahs and this kind of attitude will only leave us in bondage and at the back of the queue in the quest for progress and development. Freedom is directly linked to individual empowerment and is the only cure for the disease of over-reliance on the political function, politics, and politicians.

Freedom also implies personal responsibility and the ability to choose wisely. It is not a license. In the words of the English poet John Milton, "None can love freedom heartily, but good men; the rest love not freedom but license." The degree of latitude we are permitted in our choices depends on our ability to choose responsibly and the depth of our character as citizens. This is an area in which the African citizen has fallen horribly short. We are good at passing the buck and holding others responsible for the misery that we often find ourselves in without taking personal responsibility as African citizens. We constantly abuse our right of choice by making the wrong decisions and blaming others (e.g.

politicians,) when things go wrong.

Freedom is not to be confused with getting everything that we want. This kind of attitude betrays a sense of entitlement which is detrimental to our health and progress as a continent. In South Africa, we have a populace that mistakes freedom for getting whatever they want without contributing much and this has created a social crisis which is hindering the progress of the nation as a "disempowered" citizenry sits around and expects everything it wants to be done for it by an increasingly impotent government. As Blaise Pascal put it, "It is not good to be too free. It is not good to have everything one wants."

It is time for Africans to be truly free and to display some of the qualities and traits that are characteristic of a truly free people. It is not good enough to live in a continent where, "most of our people are so disempowered that, to them, living means not dying" to use the words of South African deputy president, Kgalema Motlanthe. This is indicative of a continent of individuals who are still in bondage. Of course, this kind of freedom can never be gotten through the exercise of outdated policies such as nationalisation and all kinds of socialist policies, because that leaves people still dependent on the state and hence not truly free.

Anti-Apartheid struggle icon Oliver Reginald Tambo said, "The fight for freedom must go on until it is won; until our country (continent) is free and happy and peaceful as part of the community of men, we cannot rest." This battle for freedom is for every individual African to take on. It is a freedom to define ourselves and our possibilities, to choose wisely, to embrace personal responsibility, to operate within the parameters of the law, to be free from over-reliance and dependence on the state and on others, to maximise our potential by looking beyond our limitations and to take charge of our individual and communal destiny as citizens instead of surrendering it to the state and politicians. As Thomas Hobbes famously said, "The power of a man is his present means to obtain some future means." This is what it means to be truly free. This is what it means to give "power to the people."

Who Needs Democracy Anyway

A couple of weeks ago I read a fascinating interview in a popular South African weekly, with Rwandan president Paul Kagame. The Kagame era has brought stability, development, and unprecedented growth to the small nation of Rwanda and has turned a fledgling country into an exemplary model for African states of how to pursue the twin goals of modernisation and economic development. This has seen Rwanda become a darling of western donor nations and increased flows of aid and investment have come into Rwanda during this period.

Amidst all of these positive developments however have emerged certain concerns about Kagame's leadership style and the increasingly authoritarian, ruthless tendencies of the Rwandan government in its dealings with any form of opposition, which culminated in the attempted murder of an exiled Rwandan general living in South Africa as well as the subsequent murder of a journalist living in Rwanda who accused the Rwandan government of being behind the attempted assassination, being blamed on Kagame's government.

Upon being questioned about the increasingly undemocratic practices of his government and the apparent lack of regard for any opposition shown by him, in the above-mentioned interview, Kagame's response was both alarming and enlightening to me. His argument seemed to be that Rwanda's main concern at this particular moment was not necessarily democracy and instilling a democratic culture, but economic growth, development, and job creation which would alleviate poverty and improve the lives of ordinary Rwandans, most of whom still live in abject poverty despite the miraculous turnaround engineered by Kagame and his regime after the genocide. To paraphrase Kagame's words from that interview, "People don't eat democracy and democracy doesn't provide people with decent living conditions and shelter."

Whilst initially alarmed by Kagame's response, the net effect was that it got me thinking about the concepts of democracy and development and the seemingly globally accepted paradigm (in a world dominated by the Washington Consensus) that democracy precedes development and is a pre-condition for economic growth and development. Having just recently completed a course on political development, where the underlying assumption seemed to be that democracy is the highest point of political development in any society and where democracy was presented as a necessary pre-condition for economic development, I found myself asking a lot of questions which had no simplistic answers but which are pertinent to us in the developing world as we seek to modernise and industrialise in the twenty-first century.

Should we seek to build and entrench democracy as a pre-requisite to economic growth and development or are our immediate socio-economic challenges so urgent that we need to focus on addressing them even at the expense of democracy and a democratic culture? Is democracy all that it is cut out to be anyway? What good is democracy if the socio-economic needs of the people are not met anyway? It was the legendary South American liberator and revolutionary Simon Bolivar who said that "the most perfect system is the one that produces the greatest possible happiness, the greatest degree of social safety and the greatest stability." What if the pursuit of democracy does not produce the social and political stability that is needed to create an environment that is conducive to economic growth and development? A glance at some of the Asian Tiger economies that have industrialised in the last sixty years or so would seem to disprove the accepted paradigm that democracy and development are inextricably linked. There are sufficient case studies in the newly industrialised Asian countries to show that growth and development are possible even in a country with an autocratic, closed political system and culture and one could argue that even in Europe, democracy and the democratic culture were an outcome of industrialisation and economic development instead of being a pre-condition for growth and development.

It would seem that the necessary conditions for growth and

development that will benefit the majority in a state are: political stability, bureaucratic efficiency, effective government, social cohesion, and visionary leadership, all of which can be created even in a non-democratic culture. The fundamental idea of democracy is to give "power to the people" but one could argue that the effects of democracy have been the exact opposite. The English philosopher Thomas Hobbes said that "the power of a man is his present means to obtain some future apparent good."

Looking at the world around us we see many examples where democracy has not necessarily enhanced the ability of the masses to obtain some future common good through improving their present means, but instead has done this for an elite minority. The Greek philosophers always viewed democracy as rule by the majority, hence Aristotle's words, "Democracy is when the indigent, and not the men of property, are the rulers." This is a perception that is still held and promoted today, even though empirical evidence proves otherwise. Most democracies in the world are nothing but oligarchies, geared towards the promotion of the interests of elite minorities even as they are masked as representing "people's power" and they leave marginalised majorities with the same sentiments as those expressed by the poet Langston Hughes, "I swear to the Lord, I still can't see why democracy means everybody but me."

Whilst proponents of democracy often hold it up as the best safeguard for the promotion and upholding of human rights, the reality is that democracy often leads to the rights of the elite minority being upheld even at the expense of impoverished majorities, a phenomenon described so perfectly by Plato in his Republic, "I say that right is the same thing in all states, namely the interest of the established ruling class; this ruling class is the strongest element in each state, and so if we argue correctly we see that right is always the same, the interest of the stronger party."

In South Africa, whilst the middle class, the economic elite, the political elite, and the opposition often express concern about the ruling party and its apparent lack of respect for democratic

25

principles, the majority keep voting the ruling party back into power. After all, ruling party politicians seem to have a greater understanding of the simple fact that impoverished majorities are not primarily concerned with democracy and democratic principles because "you can't eat democracy" as Paul Kagame put it. This understanding has enabled the ruling elite to plunder state resources for personal gain whilst operating in a "democratic culture" and pretending to represent mass interests. The question that needs to be asked is the question that was asked by Venezuela's Hugo Chavez upon careful analysis of Venezuelan society, "what kind of democracy is this that enriches a minority and impoverishes the majority?"

As I reflected upon these things after reading the Kagame interview, I found myself with even more questions than answers. With all our developmental needs as a nation that is trying to modernise and industrialise, should we be primarily concerned with entrenching and upholding democratic principles in society or are there more pressing concerns? Does democracy give "power to the people" or is it just another form of social organisation that promotes the exploitation of the masses under the guise of empowering them? Do our developmental needs require a democratic framework to be met? Is there anything beyond democracy? All these thoughts and questions arise from one simple interview. Who needs democracy anyway?

A World Without Politicians

Earlier this week as I was typically beginning my morning by spending a couple of hours reading the local and international papers online, I read a story which got me thinking about the role of politicians in society. The story was about British parliamentarians in the House of Commons who had gone to a sitting in parliament to vote on an important budgetary vote under the influence of alcohol. The worst thing was that this binge drinking had been footed by the British taxpayer and some of these parliamentarians had been so drunk that they couldn't even exercise their right to vote on this important issue.

I immediately began to think about our parliamentarians here in South Africa and some of the scandals they have been involved in over the years and it dawned on me that politicians the world over are just basically the same. Whether it is a democratic system or a closed, authoritarian system it seems that politicians the world over tend to abuse their position within society and to forget the responsibility that they have to account for their actions to the members of society. The questions that arose in my mind were the following: how much value do politicians actually add to society? If we were to do a cost/benefit analysis of politicians and their role in society would the benefits even outweigh the costs? Does society even need politicians in the first place? Is it possible to organise society in such a manner that the political function becomes redundant?

Now these may sound like absurd questions given how the world is structured at the moment with politics and politicians at the centre of society but as Albert Camus said, "the absurd is the essential concept and the first truth." Maybe we need to think of a different way to structure and organise society where there is no need for politicians and the political function because a look around the world seems to show that the contribution of politicians to a society's well-being is often minimal when compared to the cost to society of the political function. Can we imagine and create a world without politicians to run society more efficiently and effectively?

In the words of Simon Bolivar, "All history indicates that gangrenous politicians will not cure themselves with palliatives." Given this reality maybe we need to rethink some of the assumptions we have inherited and become accustomed to in terms of politics and the role of politicians in society. Can we create a post-politician society that runs efficiently and still delivers all the necessary services that are essential to society without incurring all the costs we currently incur to keep the political function at the centre of society? This may sound like a ludicrous suggestion, but a study of history will show that concepts such as democracy, market capitalism, political parties, elections etc. weren't always in existence and only came into being at a certain point in history introduced by certain individuals or particular groups of people. As the French Philosopher Michel de Montaigne put it, "How many things we held yesterday as articles of faith which today we tell as fables." Just because the current paradigm allows for politicians to play a central role in the organisation of society does not mean that this cannot change and that there is no better way to do things than what we are currently seeing.

How much value do politicians add to society? What contribution do they make which gives them so much power and makes them irreplaceable? The main problem with the current paradigm is that it purports to represent "people's power" and yet if you look the world over, whatever political system is in place, you see "people of power" (politicians) being the main point of reference instead of the "power of the people" being the main reference point. This is a curious situation as it is the people who pay the politicians through their taxes and yet the politicians have more power than those whom they work for. With politicians in charge is the taxpayer getting real value for money in terms of services rendered and quality of work or could there be a better way which would give us more value for money without relying on politicians? Now these are all questions that I believe we need to ask ourselves as Africans if we are going to progress in the twenty-first century because a glance at our post-independence history will reveal that it is African political elites who have destroyed Africa and kept her from fulfilling her immense potential.

The words of Kwame Nkrumah, "Seek ye first the political kingdom and all other things will be added to you, " have proven to be a false prophecy as far as Africa is concerned. If anything, it is the pursuit of the political kingdom to attain "all other things" that has led to Africa being plundered by political elites for personal gain. For too long we have looked to politicians to solve our problems and to direct society when they have been the bottleneck that has kept us from developing. We have embraced this slave mentality for too long. In the words of the American poet Ezra Pound, "A slave is one who waits for someone to come and free him." We have waited too long and trusted too much in political messiahs when the truth is that they are a large part of the current problem. As stated earlier this is not a phenomenon that is unique to Africa alone but one which can be seen the world over.

Can we free ourselves and come up with a new paradigm for the twenty-first century, a paradigm that takes away the role of politicians? Can we as Africans take the lead in this conversation and be the pioneers of this new form of societal organisation? We need to ask these questions and challenge the status quo if we are going to lead the world in this century. In the words of American leadership guru John Maxwell, "The willingness to ask questions coupled with the discipline to seek out answers separates leaders from followers. Influencers question assumptions, inquire about the environment around them, and probe into the future. They have an insatiable appetite to learn, and they convert their knowledge to action at light speed." Can we as Africans be the leaders, the influencers in this regard by bequeathing to the world a new way of doing things not reliant on politics and politicians but geared towards returning real power to the people and wrestling it away from parasitic political elites? As Walt Whitman, the American poet said, "A great city (nation) is that which has the greatest men and women." In other words, a great nation is built on great individual citizens, not necessarily great politicians and political leaders.

May we not continue to be like the people described by Robert Tressell in that classic novel of his, The Ragged Trousered Philanthropists, "it seemed that the majority had become so convinced of their own intellectual inferiority that they did not dare to rely on their own intelligence to guide them, preferring instead to resign the management of their affairs unreservedly into the hands of those who battered upon and robbed them...... they did not know the causes of their poverty, they did not want to know, they did not want to hear. All they desired was to be left alone so that they might continue to worship and follow those who took advantage of their simplicity and robbed them of the fruits of their toil, their old leaders, the fools or scoundrels who fed them with words, who had led them into the desolation where they now seemed to be content to grind out treasure for their masters. It was as if a flock of foolish sheep placed themselves under the protection of a pack of ravenous wolves."

It was strange to me that ordinary people looked towards governments and politicians to take them out of the mess that was the recent global economic crisis when the truth was that the crisis had been caused by the collusion between political and business elites in the first place. Too often we are just "a flock of sheep that has chosen to place itself under the protection of a pack of ravenous wolves (politicians)."

We disempower ourselves by looking to politicians to come up with the solutions to most of our problems in society and they in turn exploit our naivety to promote their personal gain. We become lazy as citizens because we leave everything in the hands of the politicians. This is a fatal mistake as politicians the world over have proven to be untrustworthy and unreliable. In South Africa, everyone in society seems to look towards politicians to solve all our problems and this has crippled us as a nation. It has bred a lazy, apathetic, disempowered populace which seems incapable of doing anything for itself unless the politicians initiate and lead. This has allowed the politicians to run amok and to enrich themselves under the guise of serving the interests of the citizenry and we have no one to blame but ourselves for this state of affairs. We have given politicians the leadership role in society without questioning their effectiveness and trying to come up with a better system.

In asking all these questions and proposing that we start looking at creating a society that does not need politicians I am not in any way calling for anarchism and I am aware that I have not proposed any solutions, just posed certain questions. My aim in doing this is to do what was proposed by Michel Foucault, "the work of an intellectual is not to mould the political will of others, it is through the analyses he does, to re-examine evidence and assumptions, to shake up habitual ways of working and thinking, to dissipate conventional familiarities, to re-evaluate rules and institutions and to participate in the formation of a political will (where he has his role as a citizen to play.)" Can we re-examine and re-evaluate the role of politicians in society? Can we come up with a different system that does away with or minimizes the role of politics and politicians in society? Can we dare to stretch our thinking, to break out of our paradigm to see if we can come up with something better and more efficient? Can we imagine a world without politicians? Can we create a world without politicians with greater efficiency, benefit and effectiveness and a lower cost to society?

Adam Smith, Capitalism and Morality

With the current debate going on in South Africa about nationalisation and the role of the state in the economy, a lot has been said about the evils of capitalism and the need for an alternative that guarantees the welfare of society as a whole. Of course, the current global economic position and the apparent failure of the neo-liberal economic paradigm have got those of us who have a vested interest in the progress of the developing world re-examining our assumptions and looking for fresh perspectives.

With that in mind, over the past week I spent some time reading some literature from the man identified as the "father of the Classical Economic School and hence capitalism", Adam Smith. I began by reading through Smith's Theory of Moral Sentiments and then ended up reading through his seminal work, titled An Inquiry into the Nature and Causes of the Wealth of Nations which was published seventeen years after the Theory of Moral Sentiments. Both books gave me great insight into the thinking of Adam Smith and are relevant to us in our search for fresh solutions to the problems the world is faced with.

To get a proper understanding of Smith's writings it is important to get an understanding of Smith's background as an academic and a thinker. Adam Smith studied moral and political science and languages at Balliol College in Oxford, and he taught moral philosophy at Glasgow College for twelve years. After publishing the Theory of Moral Sentiments his lectures were less concentrated on ethical doctrines and more on jurisprudence and political economy.

Smith's Theory of Moral Sentiments and the Wealth of Nations presented different but complementary facets of his thinking. Moral Sentiments discussed the moral forces that restrain selfishness and bind people together in a workable society whilst the Wealth of Nations assumed the existence of a just society and showed how the individual is guided and limited by economic forces.

What struck me about Smith's writings was the emphasis on personal morality and the assumption of a just society. Smith's contemporary disciples and their neo-liberal economic assumptions have completely forgotten to highlight the importance of morality and virtue in Smith's economic thinking. They emphasise the principle of the "invisible hand", the natural liberty of the individual and laissez-faire economics at the expense of other values such as sympathy, and benevolence to restrain selfishness and the right to justice which were very important to Smith as his Theory of Moral Sentiments reveals.

Smith's "invisible hand" was not as impersonal and completely ignorant of the importance of virtue and morality as the neo-liberal school would like us to believe. Smith's version of capitalism was as concerned about social justice as it was about the pursuit of profit. Neo-liberal economic thinking with its emphasis on profit even to the detriment of morality, virtue, and social justice is as far removed from Smith's thinking as Marxism is in my books, after having read through some of his works.

Maybe we need to revisit some of Adam Smith's thinking and rework some of his ideas if we want to come up with better solutions for some of the economic problems the world is faced with. The global economic crisis was caused by neo-liberal economic thinking, which claims to have its roots in Adam Smith's writings but has completely departed from some of his core assumptions. It is important to remember that Smith was a moral philosopher and political economist, not an economist per se. It is the impersonal capitalism of the neo-liberal school that has given capitalism such a bad name in most of the developing world. After having read two of Smith's most important works I must confess that I am sold on his version of capitalism, with a few tweaks and have renewed confidence that a market-based economy need not be impersonal, driven only by greed and selfishness, without any regard for virtue, morality, and ethical conduct.

Smith highlighted the importance of conscience and morality in our application of his capitalist principles and in my view it is about high time that we did the same to save the world from its current malaise, caused by greedy capitalism. In Smith's eyes, our moral faculties prescribe rules of conduct that restrain our acts of selfishness. These rules can be regarded as commands and laws of the deity. This is not the kind of capitalism based on crass materialism, secularism, and humanism which we see today. It is capitalism with a conscience. It is the kind of capitalism which we haven't yet seen and is the hope for the world as we look for ways to reconstruct the global economy and build a more just society in the twenty-first century.

Democracy Or Stability

Watching the non-violent protests that have broken out in most of North Africa and the Middle East since Tunisia's so-called Jasmin Revolution led to the fall of Ben Ali's government, got me thinking about the twin concepts of democracy and stability. Is democracy a prerequisite for social stability? If it isn't, is democracy more important than social stability?

These questions arose as I was watching a panel of experts on a news program, discussing the West's support for authoritarian regimes and dictatorships in North Africa and the Middle East under the guise of promoting social stability. The panel in question was highlighting the West's hypocrisy in seemingly promoting democracy and democratic values when it suits them and their interests but also at the same time being willing to prop up, support, and even defend non-democratic, autocratic regimes when it suits their interests.

In North Africa and the Middle East, the West has defended and propped up authoritarian regimes claiming that this is the only way to ensure social stability and guard against Islamic extremists and Fundamental Islam taking control and ruining society. This is the excuse that the West used to support Ben Ali's brutal regime in Tunisia, Hosni Mubarak's autocratic rule in Egypt and many other like-minded regimes in the region. So, it would seem to indicate that the West, by its actions, is conveying the message that social stability is more important than developing and entrenching a democratic culture as well as upholding democratic values.

Or maybe the real message here is that democracy only works when it protects and promotes Western interests. This would explain why the West supported the Algerian government and its military when they abruptly stopped run-off elections in the 1990s when it seemed obvious that the elections would bring a fundamentalist Islamic party into power. It would also explain why the West was quick to place heavy sanctions on Palestine and the Palestinian Authority when the fundamentalist Islamic party Hamas won Palestine's first democratic elections in an election that was both free and fair. In both instances democracy delivered an outcome that was unfavourable to the West and as such the West found itself engaging in anti-democratic practices all for the sake of promoting "social stability."

Another great example of this is Haiti, where the West has been happy to allow former dictator Jean-Claude "Baby Doc" Duvalier to return to the country, whilst refusing permission for Haiti's only democratically elected leader, Jean-Bertrand Aristide to return claiming that this would "destabilise" the country even though he was removed from office by a western-backed military coup after winning a clear majority in democratic elections and still remains Haiti's most popular political leader.

So, the West slams certain regimes for being authoritarian and undemocratic, like Iran but at the same time, it supports authoritarian and undemocratic regimes like Egypt on the basis that this promotes social stability. So, it would appear from the West's contradictory actions that it values stability much more than democracy or could it just be that the West values protecting its economic interests more than democracy and protecting the rights of the people in non-Western countries?

Looking at other parts of the African continent one can see many instances where the promotion of democracy has created chaos in society, brought instability and accentuated divisions and the lack of political consensus that comes because of this push for democracy and pluralism has led to civil war and the complete collapse of the nation-state project. So, even from a merely pragmatic perspective when trying to build a nation-state and create the social cohesion and consensus that are necessary for economic growth, development and progress to occur, it is sometimes necessary to subvert democracy and build on an autocratic model of governance. This would explain the success and miraculous economic turnaround of autocratic countries such as Vietnam and China which are modernising quickly and developing rapidly because of the social stability that has been attained and retained through autocracy.

This is not in any way suggesting that an autocratic model of governance is better than a democratic model, but merely stating the reality that when faced with a choice between democracy and social stability a country may be better served by choosing stability even at the cost of democracy, a democratic culture and democratic values to create the conditions necessary for economic growth, development, and progress to occur.

Family And Morality as Economic Measures

This week I thought I would write an article on an issue that I have been thinking about for the last month or so, which is the importance of family and morality in ensuring and safeguarding the economic well-being of a nation. A strong family unit and a focus on individual moral development are fundamentally important if a nation is going to develop and progress economically.

Often, we look at the Newly Industrialised Countries of the Asian bloc and we marvel at their productivity and examine their economic policies in the hope that we can learn something that will help us in our quest for development and growth on the African continent, but we tend to overlook the core qualities that pervade these societies which have made industrialisation and modernisation a reality in these nations. These are qualities such as the strict and disciplined lifestyle of the average citizen in these nations, a culture that promotes and encourages disciplined family values and a strong work ethic that dominates society. These are the kinds of things which African nations have neglected to focus on, to their detriment, in the quest for economic growth and development.

Not only is the family the basic social unit, but it is also the most fundamental economic force in society, the key to work, consumption, savings, investment, and the whole future thrust of any nation. Consequently, the continued assault on traditional family values may well be more destructive to our economic well-being as a continent than any of our faulty fiscal and monetary policies. In South Africa, the breakdown of the traditional family unit has necessitated the creation of an unsustainable welfare state, with social grants and state-driven social programmes being used to meet socio-economic needs, that in a healthy society would have been addressed within the confines of the traditional family unit. A renewed focus on building strong, productive family units is essential if the continent of Africa is going to meet its developmental objectives. The African concepts of Ujamaa (familyhood) and Harambee (pulling together) could be very important in this regard. To further highlight the importance of building strong, productive family units in the quest for economic growth, note how economists will use measures such as "household debt" and "household savings" etc. as macro measures to gauge the health of a country's economy. As Robert Kennedy so eloquently put it, "GNP (Gross National Product) measures neither the health of our children, the quality of their education, nor the joy of their play, it measures neither the beauty of our poetry nor the strength of our marriages. It pays no heed to the intelligence of our public debate or the integrity of our public officials. It measures neither our wisdom nor our learning, neither our compassion nor our devotion to our country. It measures everything in short, except that which makes life worth living, and it can tell us everything about our country except those things that make us proud to be a part of it."

As well as focusing on building strong, stable family units, African countries also need to promote and prioritise moral development if we want to see greater economic growth and development on the continent. This is especially significant because without a civilising force of universal moral standards, particularly values such as honesty, trust, self-respect, integrity, and loyalty, the marketplace quickly degenerates. A society that has no values will not produce much value. A nation whose values are declining should not be surprised at a declining economy, because the market and the world of commerce are simply the expression of human evaluation, community and solidarity-people bringing talents and abilities to the service of others through exchange.

In Africa, it is self-evident that because of our decline in values, our economies are paying an enormous price in terms of lost productivity and higher social costs. Corruption, greed, laziness, crime, violence etc. continue to prevent Africa from achieving its economic goals and unless we focus on individual moral development amongst our citizenry and leadership, we will keep falling short in this regard. In the words of Ralph Waldo Emerson, "A dollar is not value, but representative of value, and, at last, of moral values." So, right at the heart of all commercial activity is the issue of morality and values whether we are consciously aware of it or not. It takes serious self-discipline to contribute more than we take. Africa is filled with citizens and leaders who take more than they are willing to contribute. The epidemic of crime in both offices and streets on the African continent is far more indicative of our economic ills than we care to admit-not merely for the direct damage that is done to victims, but for what it says about the values and morals that are held and promoted across the continent.

In Western countries, there is growing interest in "subjective well-being." Increased wealth has ceased to bring greater happiness; a wider set of concerns, including health and quality of personal relationships, contribute to subjective well-being at least as much as higher income does. There is only so much an economic system or a set of economic policies can do for society. Economic policy frameworks and objectives can never be substitutes for higher cultural and moral commitments. We must permit freedom in the choice of buying and investing, and work on the spiritual and cultural level to inspire people toward reordering the conscience to take account of ethical ends. This is one of the keys to sustainable economic growth on the continent. It is not enough to just educate our populace, to focus on developing core skills that are necessary for a thriving economy, without focusing on morality and moral development. The global economic crisis was a good example of what happens when highly skilled, highly competent, and educated people are allowed to dictate the patterns and trends of an economy, without any focus on morality and values. It was highly educated, competent people who put the world economy in a financial mess owing to greed, corruption and the pursuit of wealth at any cost. This reminds one of the words uttered by the classical Greek philosopher, Socrates, "Are you not ashamed that you give your attention to acquiring as much money as possible, and similarly with reputation and honour, and give no attention or thought to truth and understanding the perfection of your soul?" It is the predominance of imperfect, undeveloped souls that is our greatest hindrance as a continent in terms of meeting our economic goals.

Africa needs a renewed focus on building strong, stable families and producing morally advanced citizens and leaders if we are going to see the continent achieve its growth and developmental objectives in the twenty-first century. This is a strategic imperative for the future long-term economic good of the continent and its people. We'll let the French philosopher Michel de Montaigne have the final say in this regard, "to compose our character is our duty, not to compose books, and to win, not battles and provinces, but order and tranquillity in our conduct. Our great and glorious masterpiece is to live appropriately. All other things, ruling, hoarding, building, are only little appendages and props, at most."

Progress

Looking at the current global position reminded me again of the truism that states that, "the more things change, the more they remain the same." History has a funny way of repeating itself and the world seems to go round and round until we come back to the position we started in, in the first place.

The nineteenth century began with great hope and expectancy that humanity had progressed and developed so much that man had finally come to a place where he could solve all his problems through the exercise of reason and scientific discovery. It was an age of extraordinary and rapid change. People believed in progress and the future. It was an age of expansion and transition. The world had moved from a Greek-inspired view of a static, unchanging universe to a Hegel-inspired view of an evolving and progressing world.

Of course, history records that all of this proved to be nothing but a false dawn. From the optimism of the 19th century, we entered the 20th century which was the bloodiest century ever in the history of mankind, with two World Wars and countless numbers of revolutions all over the world which claimed many innocent human lives. More people died in the last century through war and revolution, than had died cumulatively in the previous 19 centuries. So, the Age of Enlightenment and progress ended up being nothing but a damp squib.

The early part of the 21st century has begun with renewed optimism that we can create a better world, with greater co-operation and solidarity between nations. It has been a time of great technological progress and invention. The world has become increasingly linked and rapid changes are occurring in the global geopolitical sphere with new powers and alliances emerging. Yet again we stand on the precipice, with the hope that humanity is progressing and evolving, that the world can become better and that we can solve all our problems through greater cooperation. How realistic is this though?

A glance at history shows that despite great scientific discoveries, technological progress, and incredible inventions, man still faces the same problems that he has always faced. Nothing has really changed. Each generation faces the same challenges. Different faces, different levels of comfort yet similar problems. Why is this so? Because despite the great advances that have enabled us to largely master our external environment, man still has not found a way to master himself. Despite all the great changes that have made life more comfortable, man's nature remains the same. We have found a way to change everything around us, yet we don't know how to change ourselves. This is the fundamental problem that has caused conflict right throughout history.

Until we can find a mechanism, a method, a system, an outlook that will change who we are fundamentally then we will keep going around in circles, facing the same problems and battling to come up with workable solutions. Man is doomed to repeat the same mistakes unless he can find a way to transform himself, to change his very nature, the core of who he is. This is the challenge that we are faced with if this century is ever going to be any different from what has come before. Every problem that you can think of that we are faced with today can be traced back to the fundamental challenge of the problem of human nature. As the Switchfoot song goes (and I paraphrase here), "You can tell that we are the issue. It's our condition. We are ammunition. We are ammunition."

Sovereignty Versus Common Responsibility

An interesting debate that has arisen out of the recent crisis in Egypt has been the issue of national sovereignty versus common responsibility. Egyptian President Hosni Mubarak and the NDP elite in Egypt claimed that they resented foreign interference in the affairs of a sovereign state, Egypt. Having heard the same argument being used by other African leaders who refuse to relinquish power whilst brutalising their citizens, such as Robert Mugabe, Laurent Gbagbo, Sani Abacha etc, I began to wonder whether national sovereignty should always take precedence over our common responsibility to each other as human beings.

I was reminded of Bosnia in the 1990s and the brutality of the likes of Radovan Karadzic, Ratko Mladic, Slobodan Milosevic and the Serbs against Bosnian Muslims and Croats. What would have happened if the international community had decided to respect Serbia and Bosnia's sovereignty and left them alone to brutalise, murder and annihilate innocent Bosnian Muslim and Croat citizens? Surely there is some level of responsibility on the international community to intervene when you have a regime or political leadership that is brutalising innocent civilians, which transcends national sovereignty? It would appear to me that once a government has lost its legitimacy in the eyes of its people, then the international community has some responsibility to intervene to see that justice is done and the will of the people is upheld, even if it goes beyond the realms of upholding the principle of national sovereignty.

It was this respect for sovereignty which allowed the international community to stand by and watch whilst over eight hundred thousand Tutsis and moderate Hutus were being murdered in Rwanda. It is the same "respect" for sovereignty which has allowed Africa and the world to stand by whilst dictators such as Robert Mugabe and company have run amok, murdering innocent civilians and ruling with impunity. There has to be a point where our common responsibility to each other as human beings overrides the principle of sovereignty.

In my view, the principle of legitimacy before the people should be more important than the principle of sovereignty. If a government has lost its legitimacy before its people and yet refuses to heed the voice of the people, there must be some kind of mechanism which will allow the international community to step in and see to it that the will of the people is upheld even at the expense of national sovereignty at least temporarily. Otherwise, we are guilty of aiding and abetting tyrants, sycophants, autocrats, and dictators in brutalising their citizens through our passivity. I am aware that this is all open to abuse, like all things human, but the alternative is to sit around and do nothing whilst tyranny rules and that for me is unacceptable.

The Average Person is Foolish

The recent return of former Haitian dictator Jean-Claude "Baby Doc" Duvalier to his home country and the groundswell of support he received from ordinary Haitians got me thinking about the assumption that "human beings are rational" and the effect this has on society. As part of my university curriculum, I studied some law courses and one of the things we were taught was what they called "the reasonable person test" and the key question asked in that regard was, "What would the reasonable person have done in that situation?" As I watch the news and read different newspapers daily to keep myself informed about events around the world, I find myself questioning whether it is reasonable to assume that the average person in society is indeed reasonable.

Are human beings inherently rational and reasonable or are we more driven by emotion in our analysis and interpretation of events as they happen around us? The fact that ordinary Haitians could celebrate the return of a man who ruled with an iron fist, tortured, abused, and killed so many innocent civilians is an indicator of how irrational the average person is and how little thought is given to the people and causes the average person supports. It is ordinary citizens who we see supporting Laurent Gbagbo in the Ivory Coast and believing his rhetoric about a Western plot to oust him from the presidency. I have been even more surprised to see how many of my educated South African friends have bought into this argument.

It is ordinary South Africans who cheer for the likes of Robert Mugabe and treat him as a hero whenever he visits South Africa, even though he has butchered, murdered, and tortured so many innocent Zimbabwean citizens. All this is because of the highly emotive argument that he is at least "standing up to the West" unlike other African leaders. It was ordinary young people who turned up in droves to support Mao's diabolic "Cultural Revolution" which led to the death of millions of innocent Chinese people and spread chaos through Chinese society, only alleviated when Deng Xiaoping took over the reins in 1976. It was ordinary Germans who supported Adolf Hitler and his NAZI party, based on their emotive promises to restore German pride and by the time they woke up to the consequences of their support for so evil a man, Hitler and his cronies had plunged the world into an unnecessary war and millions of lives had been lost.

The best and most popular politicians are those who appeal to people at an emotive level and not at an intellectual, rational level. That is why South Africa's two most popular politicians of the last two years are: Jacob Zuma and Julius Malema. Love them or hate them, these two are brilliant politicians because they have figured out that the way to make it in politics and attain power is to appeal to the emotions and not the minds of the majority. That is why Sarah Palin and the "Tea Party" movement have had such a massive impact on American politics. Barack Obama's messianic "Yes We Can" political campaign, which brought him to the White House, showed a clear understanding of this aspect of human nature. Hence, he overpromised knowing he could only under-deliver, out of the knowledge that this is what people wanted to hear.

A glance at the world and history reveals that human beings seldom use reason in making key decisions and are often driven by emotion. This means that the assumption that human beings are "inherently rational and reasonable" could be one of the most dangerous assumptions to make when you are trying to order and structure society. This is the fundamental assumption on which democracies are built but we have seen democracies bring into power some of the worst despots in history owing to populist politics that appeal to people's emotions.

Because the average person is more emotive than rational, we find that whatever political system you set in place, there will always be an elite minority who are rational enough to govern an irrational, emotive majority. That is why every people's revolution that seeks to restructure society and usher in an era of greater equality and justice for all ends up either re-enforcing the power of the existing elite or producing a new elite which ends up lording it over the majority. Every revolution has been such a colossal failure when judged by its long-term effects. The celebrated French Revolution ended up falling prey to Napoleon's dictatorship, the Iranian Revolution to a dictatorship led by Islamic clerics, and the Bolshevik Revolution to a corrupt Communist elite. Because the majority are irrational and unreasonable they are open to the manipulations of a more rational, calculating, elite minority. This is what you find happening in all corners of the earth, irrespective of what kind of political system you are in.

The result is that whether in crisis times or boom times, the more rational elite minority always thrives and the irrational, emotive majority always struggles. This happens under all kinds of varied political systems. It is an inevitable fact of human existence which men across the ages have tried to change with no success at all. Maybe the primary assumption we should make when we think about how to organise and structure society is this: that the average human being is irrational and emotive, often to their detriment.

We, The People

As I was watching the "people's revolution" in Egypt and hearing analysts talking about the potential domino effect for the whole North African/Middle East area, I began to wonder about the efficacy of social revolution and whether the goals of a more just, equitable and fair society are ever attained by way of social revolution.

Webster's dictionary defines revolution as, "an overthrow or repudiation and thorough replacement of an established government or political system by the people governed or radical and pervasive change in society and their social structure." So, revolutions always aim to overthrow a government or political system with the primary goal of ushering in a new government or a new political system that will be more just, more equitable and fairer to all members of society. Revolutions always begin with the hope that the majority will get a better deal from the new system or government than what they enjoyed under the old system or government. However, when looking at the long-term effects of each social revolution that has occurred throughout history, it is difficult to see how the lot of the majority is improved via social revolution.

Eric Hoffer in his book, The True Believer states that "every great cause begins as a movement, becomes a business and eventually degenerates into a racket." So, for example, the French Revolution which began to promote, "liberty, fraternity, and equality" for all citizens ended up degenerating into anarchy and chaos which ended up taking France into a Napoleonic dictatorship. So, the sum total of the revolution was the replacement of one elite, the traditional nobility by another elite, Napoleon and his military dictatorship which oppressed the French people no less than the old establishment and ended up leaving common people in the same position they were in before.

The same result was seen in the infamous Bolshevik Revolution in the early part of the 20th century in Russia, which ended up proving Albert Camus' statement that, "all modern revolutions have ended in a reinforcement of the power of the state" to be true. A revolution that began with the aim of freeing Russia from Tsarist dictatorship with the promise of creating a more egalitarian society ended up falling prey to the brutal dictatorship of the Communist Party and produced a system and leadership which was more brutal and ruthless than that of Tsarist Russia. So, the revolution moved Russia from the dominance of one elite, the Tsarist nobility, to a new, more brutal elite, the Communist Party and its senior leadership and state bureaucrats. So, the result was that the common people were no better off in the new system than they were under the old system. This is a reality highlighted by the English author George Orwell's statement that, "no advance in wealth, no softening of manner, no reform or revolution has ever brought human equality a millimetre nearer."

So, we see that every revolution ends up having the effect of replacing one oligarchic elite that governs with its own interests in mind, with a new oligarchic elite that governs with its own interests in mind under the guise of promoting the interests of the people. The people are simply a tool that the new elite uses to replace the existing establishment to attain power and once that power is attained the new elite builds institutions and structures that safeguard its interests often at the expense of the majority. This is the result you find whatever a political system is in place, whether it's a closed political system or an open political system. This is because as Luthando Tofu put it, 'the nature of human sinfulness corrupts all forms of social contracts."

That is why the Cuban Revolution degenerated into a dictatorship, benefitting mostly the Communist elite. That is also why the post-colonial African state, established with the hope and the promise of ensuring the well-being of the African majority, ended up becoming nothing more than the personal fiefdom of the African political elite who governed with impunity and looted state coffers and resources to advance and promote their narrow sectional interests. That is what happened to post-Communist Russia where the old Communist elite where replaced by a new, oligarchic business and political elite which gained power to access and acquire state resources for personal gain and the same phenomenon has been evidenced in contemporary South African society where the post-Apartheid era has seen the emergence of a ruling-party aligned parasitic political and business elite which is concerned only with using the state and its institutions to create personal wealth for themselves.

So, we have a constant pattern throughout history where revolutionary political movements and their leaders gain access to power through "people's movements" but once that power has been attained, new institutions and structures are set in place with the primary aim of protecting and promoting the interests of a minority, parasitic elite and the interests of that minority take precedence over the interests of the impoverished majority. This seems to be the way of the world and is seemingly unavoidable no matter what political system you are in. As the old proverb goes, "It is useless for the sheep to pass resolutions in favour of vegetarianism while the wolf remains of a different nature." It is useless to put new governments and political systems in place, expecting change that will benefit the majority when the reality is that human nature has not changed and the natural inclination of most humans, despite their best intentions, is to promote personal interests and personal agendas at the expense of the majority. One could argue that even supposedly very open societies like the United States of America, have political systems and social structures that promote the interests of a wealthy elite, even at the expense of the majority and even when popular movements break out, they end up falling prey to these elite interests.

The Greek philosopher Plato idealistically stated that "our object in the construction of the state is the greatest happiness of the whole and not that of any one class." A look at history and the world we live in shows that often the state is nothing more than, "a social construct primarily for the benefit of elites" contrary to what Plato and his contemporaries envisaged. This makes one wonder whether the so-called revolutions in Tunisia, Egypt, Yemen, and many other Middle Eastern countries will produce the kind of change that we desire to see, with all the different groups in those societies benefitting from the new dispensation that will undoubtedly emerge from all the chaos that those societies are currently experiencing.

Where Is the Meaning in All This?

Two events happened in the last week or so which got me thinking about an issue that has been of primary concern to me for the best part of the last three years. Firstly, the natural disaster in Japan devastated Japan and left a trail of death and destruction which I found to be incomprehensible. Secondly, over the weekend I attended a family funeral which was deeply emotional and personal.

The death and destruction brought me back to an issue that I have grappled with over the years without necessarily coming to any concrete conclusion. It is the issue of existence and meaning. There is something about death and its finality which tends to get one reflecting on life and whether it has any meaning at all. As a philosophy student and with philosophy being an intellectual discipline which is concerned with the nature of reality and the investigation of the general principles of knowledge and existence, it is a question that has not been far from my mind when I have been delving into the works of the likes of Kant, Hegel, Rousseau, Plato, Nietzsche, Sartre etc.

As I was standing at the family funeral observing all the sadness and helplessness that comes with being faced with death and experiencing some of that sadness and helplessness myself, I couldn't help but be struck by the apparent meaninglessness of life. In the words of Shakespeare in his play, Hamlet, "What a piece of work is man! How noble in reason! How infinite in faculty! In form and moving how to express! How admirable in action! How like an angel in apprehension! How like a god! The beauty of the world! The paragon of animals! And yet, to me, what is this quintessence of dust?"

In that moment I found myself completely aware of the fickleness of human existence, the meaninglessness of all our toil and labour, the purposelessness of much of our living. We strive to accomplish so much; we toil and labour most of our lives only to find out that most of the things we have been chasing after are in the end not worth it. As American corporate legend Lee Iacocca put it, "Here I am in the twilight years of my life, still wondering what it's all about. I can tell you this, fame and fortune are for the birds." Here I was still at the early stages of my life, like Iacocca, still wondering what it was all about.

According to the Russian novelist Fyodor Dostoevsky in his novel The Possessed, "the one essential condition for human existence is that man should always be able to bow down before something infinitely great. If men are deprived of the infinitely great, they will not go on living and will die of despair. The infinite and the eternal are as essential for man as the little planet on which he dwells", or in Dostoevsky's other novel, The Brothers Karamazov, "all that man seeks on earth-that is, someone to worship, someone to keep his conscience and some means of uniting all in one unanimous and harmonising ant-heap."

Having been a student pastor at a university campus-based "mega-church" in Cape Town in another life and having done some theological studies I used to believe all this. I used to believe that the answer to the search for meaning for humanity lies in religion, specifically Christianity and in this belief in a God who created us as human beings to worship Him. Whenever I found myself faced with the question of meaning this was the answer that satisfied me and gave me a sense of purpose. I used to believe that my purpose was to live my life in such a manner that one day when I die, I will be accepted into a place called "heaven" where all the sufferings of this life come to an end and life is just pure bliss. I used to believe that my purpose in life was to partner with God in his quest to restore and redeem the world.

But at some stage, these answers ceased to be sufficient. I began to ask myself: what kind of megalomaniac of a God would create me solely so that I could keep telling him how great he is? What kind of a God would create a world that had the potential to be so messed up and then spend so much time trying to redeem it? What kind of God would create human beings, put them in a world and expect them to live with their focus on another world still to come, with the promise that the coming world would be better? Why not just put us in that world in the first place and not even bother creating the first? Not that I have stopped believing in the God of Christianity but the answers that I thought I had found in the end, have turned out to be insufficient. As William Shakespeare put it in King Lear, "like flies to wanton boys, are we to the gods. They kill us for the sport."

In the last few years, I also did some work in a poor community in Johannesburg and was faced with situations of extreme suffering, pain, and devastation almost daily as I dealt with people and I found myself asking the question at the end of each day, what is the point of all this? Where is the meaning of all this? I saw people wake up every day, dashing off to work to do the most menial of jobs just to survive and I kept asking the question, why? Most people in the world spend most of their lives in survival mode, just looking to get by and no one seems to be bothered enough to ask the question, but what's the point? How can a world where the majority spend most of their lives looking to survive make any sense to anyone? I was daily reminded of Albert Camus' words, "The gods had condemned Sisyphus to ceaselessly rolling a rock to the top of a mountain, whence the stone would fall back of its own weight. They had thought with some reason that there is no more dreadful punishment than futile and hopeless labour." A glance around the world shows that most people are living in this space.

Then I had a friend, an MD of a top company who is worth hundreds of millions, who I used to have breakfast or lunch with once a month at the Michelangelo Towers in Sandton, Johannesburg and every conversation we had always ended up veering towards the search for meaning and how empty his life was. He was no longer thrilled by concluding billion-rand deals, making more money, travelling to exotic places, buying new cars, dining at the finest places etc. He felt there was more to life, gave away a third of his money to worthy causes, was an active member of a Christian church for most of his life, and had a stable marriage, and great kids and yet he was still unfulfilled and kept coming to me to help him find, "the meaning of life."

I looked at modernity and found nothing but emptiness in that as well. As Albert Einstein put it, "the modern age has perfect means and confused ends" or in the words of T.S Eliot, "endless invention, endless experiment, brings knowledge of motion, but not stillness...where is the life we have lost in living? Where is the wisdom we have lost in knowledge?" My studies in philosophy made me aware of the fact that the issues I was grappling with were issues that thinkers throughout the ages have grappled with. We cannot get away from the fact that we are in the world and that the world is a highly complex machinery, organism or call it what we will. These facts do raise questions and the ancient thinkers were right to ask them. For a modern man to get lost in technology and become so preoccupied with aspects of the physical world that he sees nothing else is a form of intellectual obscurantism and escapism.

My philosophy studies also exposed to me the emptiness of humanism, atheism, and secularism, aptly depicted in the following statement by Alexander Pope, "know then thyself, presume not God to scan; the proper study of mankind is man." I found myself asking the humanists and atheists the same question that Ravi Zacharias asks, "If man is the measure of all things, someone has to determine which man: is it Hitler, Hugh Hefner, Stalin, or Mother Teresa?"

The myth that human meaning could be found in living sacrificially for others out of loyal devotion to some deity was exposed as just that, a myth when I read excerpts from Mother Teresa's personal diary and realised how depressed and lonely she was despite having lived such a pious, devotional, self-sacrificing life. The only conclusion I could come up with was that there was no meaning to human existence and if there is no one has yet been able to find it. Some choose to hold certain beliefs that give them moments of feeling good about themselves and their existence but during their lives, when faced with the realities of day-to-day living they are hard-pressed to find an answer to the burning question: where is the meaning in all this?

Thomas Robert Malthus, HIV/AIDS And Population Control

A few weeks ago, I found myself reading the Classical economist Thomas Robert Malthus' Essay on the Principle of Population written in 1798 and his Summary View of the Principle of Population written in 1830. This got me thinking about the problem of HIV/AIDS and the importance of population control to ensure economic health and sustainability.

Whilst Malthus' theories are highly controversial and to some extent discredited, they do hold some important lessons for those of us who live in what is termed the developing world. His writings addressed such topics as population growth, methodology of GDP accounting, value theory, land rent, and aggregate demand.

Malthus set himself the lofty goal of "accounting for much of the poverty and misery observable among the lower classes of every nation" in his writings. In his "law of population" Malthus claimed that, "the population when left unchecked increases geometrically whilst subsistence increases at best only arithmetically. "

Malthus identified two types of checks for population growth:

"preventive checks and positive checks." According to Malthus, "preventive" checks are those that reduce the birth rate. Malthus termed it moral restraint. In his view, people who could not afford children should either postpone marriage or never marry. Conduct before and during marriage should be strictly moral. The preventive check he disapproved of, Malthus called vice. This included things like prostitution and birth control, both of which reduced the birth rate.

With seventy per cent of the world's inhabitants living in developing nations and nine out of every ten people added to the world population during the years 2000-2010 being found in these countries, Malthus' theories do carry a message for us in the developing world. It is a fact of life that in the developing world there are children being born every day out of wedlock with no realistic chance of ever becoming economically active, productive citizens and instead becoming a burden to society and the world.

It is the poorest of the poor who often breed the most and often this is done with no thought to the future of the children being birthed, which simply burdens society and puts extra weight on those citizens who are the most economically productive and often the most responsible when it comes to giving birth to children. This is an unnecessary burden with massive economic consequences which could be avoided if Malthus' preventive checks were applied to the developing world.

Positive checks are those that increase the death rate, things such as famine, misery, plague, and war. Malthus elevated these to the position of natural phenomena or laws; unfortunate evils required to limit the population. In Malthus' eyes, these positive checks represented punishments for people who had not practised moral restraint. If positive checks could somehow be overcome, people would face starvation because a rapidly growing population would press upon a food supply that at best would grow slowly.

According to Malthus, poverty and misery are the natural punishment for the failure of the "lower classes" to restrain their reproduction. As a direct result, Malthus believed that there should be no government relief for the poor. In his view to give the poor aid would cause more children to survive, thereby ultimately worsening the problem of hunger.

Whilst all of this may sound Darwinian and uncaring and I don't agree with a lot of what Malthus says, there are elements of his theory which are worth noting. In a world where a large percentage of HIV-positive patients contract the virus through irresponsible sexual behaviour, the question needs to be asked whether society should be made to bear the cost of keeping alive and healthy those who didn't value their lives enough to be sexually responsible in the first place? As inconvenient truth as this is, we must realise that the majority of those who are HIV positive have contracted the virus through irresponsible sexual behaviour and are thus not victims but culprits who don't necessarily deserve our sympathy. Not to say that we should be uncaring, selfish, and apathetic, but their irresponsible sexual behaviour costs society a disproportionate amount and has socio-economic ramifications which should never be taken lightly and by treating them as victims rather than culprits we indirectly encourage this behaviour and allow the disease to spread indefinitely.

To add to that it is also true that the poor tend to reproduce unthinkingly without caring much about the cost to society and often expect and demand that society bear the burden for their irresponsibility. By treating the poor merely as victims and not making them aware that their behaviour has consequences that go beyond them, we perpetuate a continuous cycle of poverty and dependency as we are not discouraging this irresponsible behaviour. We dehumanise the poor by not treating them as rational individuals who can consider and rectify their choices and decisions when faced with bearing the consequences of their actions instead of looking to the government and society to bail them out and make decisions for them.

Where Are the Extremists Of Our Day?

Recently I was having a typically heated political discussion with an acquaintance, who expressed his genuine disappointment at some of my radical political stances of late and stopped short of calling me "mad" for some of my opinions and thoughts on South African politics at present. Said acquaintance wanted me to be more, "balanced, reasonable, and moderate" in my political opinions instead of being, "radical and extreme" as he perceived me to be. This got me thinking about the words of Corrie Ten Boom, "reasonable people conform to their environment and the world they are in, unreasonable people expect the environment they are in and their world to conform to who they are. The world changes because of unreasonable people."

I realised at that moment that being "reasonable, balanced, and moderate" has never been one of my priorities and in fact, most of the people who have changed the world and impacted history have not been of the "reasonable, balanced, and moderate type." The world-changers and history-makers are often highly unreasonable, terrifyingly extremist and dangerously radical, whether it is for a good or a bad cause. David Ben-Gurion was a man of such nature, Ayatollah Ruhollah Khomeini was a man of such nature, Martin Luther was a man of such nature, Ernesto "Che" Guevara was a man of such nature, Napoleon Bonaparte was a man of such nature, so was Shaka Zulu, Simon Bolivar, Patrice Lumumba, Trotsky, Robespierre, Marcus Garvey, and Cecil John Rhodes. History belongs to the radicals, the extremists. The ordinary person who leaves no mark on history is often the "reasonable, sensible, balanced" type.

Typically, questions began to go through my mind: if history is often influenced by radicals and extremists, why is it that society does everything within its power to make "reasonable" people out of us all? Why is it that the people who are often the most radical and the most extreme and hence who hold the most influence and shape society, are the people who are on the side of evil instead of those on the side of righteousness? To quote the words of the poet

W.B Yeats, often throughout history the problem has been that, "the best lack all conviction, while the worst are full of passionate intensity." Why is there often greater intensity, passion, focus, and radicalism amongst those who are promoting a bad cause than amongst those who are standing up for that which is just, right, and true?

I looked at my own country South Africa and its recent history and saw how a bunch of extremist, radical Afrikaner intellectuals and political leaders were able to take over this nation and direct it on a path that has had devastating consequences for its people even up to the present day. This is epitomised by the words of Hendrik Verwoerd, "I do not have the nagging doubts of ever wondering whether perhaps I am wrong." This kind of attitude, this kind of uncompromising conviction is what it takes to shape history and change the world, whether it is for good or for bad. Where were the righteous Afrikaner thinkers and political leaders who were convinced enough about the evil of Verwoerd's policy to stand up against him and present a different vision for South Africa in his day? There were probably many Afrikaner people who saw the evil in the policy of Apartheid and yet none of them had the same conviction and fortitude as Verwoerd and his crew so the voice of evil prevailed and generations were affected negatively thereafter. This kind of scene has played itself out on so many occasions at different moments, in different parts of the world, during various epochs throughout history.

Unreasonable, extremist, radical history-makers are never happy to accept things as they are, they never conform to the norms of society and they don't live according to the fatalistic attitude, "que sera sera", which is often the attitude taken by reasonable people as they watch history unfold from a spectators vantage point. Bono, of U2 fame, is one such character, "I can't live with acquiescence. I can't make peace with myself or the world. I just can't. To me, it's like rolling over. So, in doing things like Jubilee 2000, I do feel better for actively feeling that I'm getting my hands around the throat of something I care about. If I'm honest, I'm rebelling against my indifference. I am rebelling against the idea that the world is the way the world is, and there's no damned thing I can do about it. So, I'm trying to do some damned thing." This is the attitude of a world-changing, history-shaping individual. What is it going to take to get us out of our seats and onto the playing field? When will we stop watching extremist political leaders, ideologues, and demagogues destroying our nations whilst we moan and complain as mere spectators? Where are the crusaders for social justice, economic transformation, social revolution, and mass interests who have this kind of "unreasonable" passion, whose demands cannot be denied?

I am reminded of the words of Robert Mangaliso Sobukwe, uttered whilst he was still a student at Fort Hare University in the late 1940s, "watch our movements keenly and if you see any signs of "broadmindedness" or "reasonableness" in us, or if you hear us talk of practical experience as a modifier of man's views, denounce us as traitors to Africa." Are we producing students of this world-changing resolve on our university campuses? Where are the young Sobukwes of our time who will take our nation and our continent forward?

Do we have statesmen of the ilk of Nigeria's founding father, Nnamdi Azikiwe, who fought against the colonialist power of his day with such revolutionary zeal that it was no surprise that he was able to lead Nigeria to independence, "tell a man whose house is on fire to give a moderate alarm, tell a man moderately to rescue his wife from the arms of a ravisher; tell a mother to extricate gradually her babe from the fire into which it has fallen; but do not ask me to use moderation in a cause like the present." Who will fight the battle for economic emancipation for Africa's peoples, the war against poverty and unjust inequality with similar conviction and unwavering confidence?

Where are the businesspeople in our nation that will swim against the tide of BEE, the entitlement mentality and the exploitation of state tendering processes to enrich themselves at society's expense, but will instead become the entrepreneurial class that this nation needs to solve some of its socio-economic problems? Where are the J. Paul Gettys of South Africa, "the totally successful businessman is essentially a dissenter, a rebel who is seldom if ever satisfied with the status quo. He creates success by constantly seeking new and better ways to do and make things?"

Where are the Martin Luther King Juniors of this continent when it comes to moral leadership that drives society forward and takes us away from racial, ethnic, tribal, and religious divisions which often polarise us and produce all sorts of social unrest, civil strife, and civil wars which have devastated this continent and kept it from developing? Upon being accused by his detractors of being an extremist, here is how Martin Luther King Junior responded, "was not Jesus an extremist for love: love your enemies, bless them that curse you, do good to them that hate you, and pray for them which despitefully use you and persecute you? Was not Amos an extremist for justice: Let justice roll down like waters and righteousness like an ever-flowing stream? Was not Paul an extremist for the Christian gospel: I bear in my body the marks of the Lord Jesus? Was not Martin Luther an extremist: Here I stand; I cannot do otherwise, so help me God? And John Bunyan: I will stay in jail till the end of my days before I make a butchery of my conscience. And Abraham Lincoln: Thus, this nation cannot survive half slave and half free. And Thomas Jefferson: we hold these truths to be self-evident, that all men are created equal... So, the question is not whether we will be extremists, but what kind of extremists we will be, will we be extremists for hate or love?"

This generation of Africans needs to answer this question and answer it soon if Africa is going to be turned around: what kind of extremists will we be? Will we be extremists for corruption, violence, greed, racial disunity, ethnic hatred, closed society, authoritarian society, passive citizenship, economic injustice, irresponsibility, and blame-shifting as the previous generations were? Or will we be extremists for economic justice, inclusiveness, unity, reconciliation, civil responsibility, open society, a democratic culture, productivity, industry, and enterprise as opposed to welfare living, as our current situation demands if we are ever going to emerge from the doldrums as a continent? What shall it be oh Africa? Shall we continue in our passivity?

Where are the extremists for just causes in our day? We know that the extremists who stand for evil causes have had their day in Africa and it is now time for the "best to be full of passionate intensity" just as the worst were in previous African generations.

2

Pub Conversations

Black Business Has Failed Us

A couple of weeks ago I was at the local Irish Pub enjoying a few rounds of Namibia's finest export. I ended up in an intense conversation with two of the pub regulars who happened to be sitting with me. One was a hotshot executive in one of South Africa's biggest banking groups and the other was a successful businessman. As is often the case when you have conversations with black South Africans who are in the corporate sector or are running their own business, we started off talking about the lack of transformation amongst South African corporates, with both of them sharing stories of ridiculous window-dressing by corporates in order to appear to be transforming whereas the actual reality is that nothing much has changed after almost two decades of black majority rule.

Whilst these sentiments were not new to me as I hear them in almost every conversation I have with black corporates, there was a sentiment expressed by one of these guys that deviated from the status quo and piqued my interest. This was the sentiment that "black business has failed the people of South Africa." It all began with a critique of black organisations like the Black Management Forum (BMF), which was accused of being nothing more than a tool for certain black corporates to position themselves for key positions within the South African corporate sector and once this has been achieved those individuals then forget about the issues that affect the rest of black South Africa. He contrasted this with organisations like Afriforum, die Afrikaanse Handelsinstituut etc. which are clear in their promotion of the interests of Afrikaner people and their culture and not just certain individuals within that people group as we see in black organisations like the BMF.

The conversation then moved on to the issue of the failure of successful black businesspeople to invest in black communities: to help build infrastructure, deliver quality education, and improve services. The issue raised was that we are not seeing black businesspeople adopting for example one or two poorly performing schools in the townships or the rural areas, paying highly qualified and skilled teachers to go and teach in these schools, building sports facilities and other infrastructure that is necessary to enhance the learning experience and improving the governance and administration of these schools in order to ensure better overall results. What we are seeing instead is black businesspeople aggressively chasing profits and wealth at whatever cost without contributing as much as they could to address the developmental needs of the country. A lot of the time we see the same businesspeople pushing for the government to enforce employment equity and affirmative action legislation because it benefits them and their narrow sectional interests, without in any way contributing to improving the lot of the impoverished black majority.

Contrast this with Afrikaner businesspeople and the contribution they made to the development of Afrikaner people once the National Party had taken over the running of the country in 1948. Contrary to popular opinion there is nothing wrong with prominent black businesspeople using their political connections to grow their businesses and improve their profits. This is exactly how great Afrikaner entrepreneurs like Anton Rupert emerged and became extremely wealthy, however, the significant difference has been that they invested in education, cultural initiatives etc that contributed to the development of their people, whilst using the state and their connections to the National Party to build their wealth, whereas we are not seeing the same level of commitment from black business in contemporary South Africa.

Even in contemporary times Afrikaner business people like Johan Rupert, Christo Wiese, the Wessels family (Toyota SA), Laurie Dippenaar, and G.T Ferreira (First Rand group) etc. still contribute significantly to cultural and educational initiatives that contribute to the development of Afrikaner people and this is something that they prioritise and value, but we are not seeing the same kind of commitment from black business to the impoverished black majority in South Africa.

Whilst this may seem to be completely harsh on black businesspeople, it is a historical fact that society is reliant on the contribution of its more affluent citizens to progress and develop. In the United States of America, we find that many of the great entrepreneurs who contributed greatly to the country's economic success were aware of this reality and hence embraced their responsibility to society. Great entrepreneurs like John D. Rockefeller, Cornelius van der Bilt, Andrew Carnegie, J.P Morgan, Jay Gould etc are remembered not just for the wealth they accumulated but for their contribution to the development of American society in diverse fields. They contributed to enhancing American education by building universities and schools, building libraries and cultural centres (or at least funding them), setting up bursary and endowment schemes, preserving and promoting America's diverse and rich cultural heritage by being patrons of the arts etc. These are the kinds of contributions that we saw and still see from Afrikaner businesspeople towards the development of their people and hence the Afrikaner people have progressed immensely over the last hundred years but sadly this is sorely lacking when it comes to black business and its commitment to black people.

No less a ruthless businessman and capitalist than John D. Rockefeller (probably the greatest businessman that has ever lived) said, "if I have no other achievement to my credit than the accumulation of wealth, then I have made a poor success of my life." This is a lesson that black businesspeople and corporates need to learn. Too often all black businesspeople are concerned about their enrichment, even if it comes at the expense of the rest of society. We need to start demanding more from black business. What contribution is black business making to the improvement of education in our country for example? How much is black business investing in impoverished black communities so we can see more development? What is black business doing to try and help address the housing backlog in our country? What infrastructure is black business building in poor black communities to improve the quality of life for the average black South African and create better conditions for the success of our people?

These are all questions that need to be posed to black business in South Africa. Black business is often very quick to run to the government to ask it to enact and enforce legislation that will ensure transformation, greater equity, and increased ownership for black people in the economy, but we need to ask ourselves: what benefit has this been to the impoverished majority really? Black business needs to learn from Afrikaner business which from the early days of the Nats, used its government connections to increase its profits but in turn, invested in the Afrikaner people and hence we see the tremendous development of the Afrikaner nation.

Black business needs to heed the words of another great American entrepreneur, Harvey Firestone (Firestone Rubber), "a man who isn't willing to share his success with others won't have much success to put in his own pocket." Black business needs to share its success with the majority of impoverished black South Africans by investing in black communities and helping to improve the quality of education that young black people are receiving in impoverished communities.

Mandela Sold Us Out

The Julius Malema hate speech trial has served to expose how truly divided we are as a nation and how fickle this "rainbow" that supposedly makes up our nation truly is.

During the trial proceedings, it became blatantly obvious that South Africa is no more united and reconciled now than it was during the 1980s, at the height of Apartheid. On the one hand, we had Afriforum and its legal counsel, who purport to represent the Afrikaner nation and its fears in a united South Africa and on the other hand we had Julius Malema with his unique brand of populism, which the media has mistaken for African Nationalism, purporting to represent the impoverished black majority, who make up a large percentage of the population in South Africa.

The Afrikaner group was still using the terminology of the 1980s in its cross-examination of Malema, exposing fears of: "die swart gevaar", "die rooi gevaar" and such outdated concepts which have no place in a united South Africa. They even had the audacity to claim that there was a deliberate, state-sponsored genocide against Afrikaners occurring in South Africa today.

Malema in his testimony sought to portray himself as some kind of modern-day revolutionary, challenging an unjust system that seeks to subjugate the black South African and entrench white hegemony, as has always been the case in South Africa. He sought to justify the singing of a song which for all intents and purposes had its place in the South Africa of the 1980s but has no place in the South Africa of the twenty-first century that we are presently trying to construct.

The sad reality of this whole saga was that it was an accurate reflection of the fears of most white South Africans as well as the anger and resentment of a large proportion of black South Africans. White South Africans feel they are being strategically forced out of the new South Africa; Black South Africans feel that white South Africans are still stuck in the old South African mindset of "baaskaap." Malema and Afriforum simply represent the two strands.

So here we are almost two decades after our "miraculous" transition, still stuck on race issues and instead of disappearing, they seem to be growing more prominent with each week that goes by. One need only listen to the commentary of most ordinary South Africans on our popular radio and television shows as well as read the comments section of most of our newspapers to verify this.

We keep talking past each other. We rarely if ever truly listen to one another. When it comes down to it most of the public discourse in South Africa is informed by race and racial issues. We try to paper over it, but it keeps cropping up. At my local watering hole in Fourways Johannesburg, we have a group of pub regulars who come to the pub each day, after work for a few cold ones and some camaraderie. This group is known as the "pub family." It is made up of people of all kinds: rich, poor, black, white, Indian, and Coloured. This is a group that gets along and has loads of fun together and is in many ways a great reflection of what South Africa should be, but last week when I was at the pub, we started discussing the Malema trial and suddenly, the group was divided along racial lines.

The whites who make up the "pub family" seemed to take one side on this particular political issue whilst the darkies were united in their support of Juju and his views as expressed at the trial. This would be alright if it wasn't a reflection of broader South African society. We may get along, work together, live in the same neighbourhood and even drink at the same spot together but when push comes to shove, and political issues are put to the fore we always reveal how truly divided we are as a nation.

Now the world celebrated the "miracle" of the birthing of the Rainbow Nation and the reconciliation effort spearheaded by Nelson Mandela amongst many but in truth, this was all a facade. It was a false reconciliation. South Africans have never been truly reconciled and all Nelson Mandela did was defer the exposure of racial tension and racial issues to a later period. For doing that Mandela was acclaimed as a saint by the world and lauded as some kind of superhuman messiah, but from the context of what we are seeing in South Africa today, it may be fair to say that Nelson Mandela sold us out. He got glory and critical acclaim for spearheading a reconciliation which never truly was and now that he has gone "the chickens are truly coming home to roost" and it is not a pretty picture. Perhaps we need to revisit Mandela's place in our history as a nation. Instead of acclaiming him as some sort of saint who brought us together and helped create a nation out of the rubble of a divided past, maybe we should see Mandela for what he truly was/is: a great charmer, a figurehead who purported to unite us, whilst in reality, all he was doing was deferring our racial tensions for a later period when he wouldn't be around to deal with the fallout. For this the world applauded him and we foolishly marched behind him not realising that issues that get swept under the carpet without being dealt with head-on, have a habit of coming out at the most inopportune of times as we are seeing with the growing racial tensions in present-day South Africa.

A World of Takers

I have recently started frequenting a quaint little pub in Bryanston in the north of Johannesburg, South Africa which has a lot of English patrons. It is a great place to enjoy a few pints of Guinness or some Irish whisky under the African sun after a long day at work.

Since I started frequenting this pub, I have noticed that these English expats who make up a large proportion of the customer base of this pub spend most of their time at the pub not only drinking copious amounts of alcohol as is the English tradition but also whingeing and complaining about South Africa and Africa and making fun of the continent and its "stupid" leaders as they are wont to call them. They never get enough of complaining about the corruption within the ruling party in South Africa, the high crime levels mostly the fault of black South Africans and in fact as one of them recently told me, " I came to South Africa thirteen years ago with lots of optimism, hoping to experience the Rainbow Nation, but after having been a victim of crime once too often and having seen the racist policies of the ruling party I have become a bigot and have begun to detest everything that is represented by ANC-led South Africa."

Being an understanding sort of chap (or at least I'd like to think I am) I was happy to let all this slide until I pitched up at the pub in my ANC cap last week and one of the English patrons took offence and began to voice his displeasure at the fact that I had come wearing an ANC cap. I avoided making a big issue out of the whole thing but left there reflecting on the irony that an Englishman, who had left his home country to come and live in South Africa and was enjoying a great life on the southern tip of Africa was coming down hard on me for wearing a cap with the ruling party logo on it. This would have been fine if it was an isolated incident but through my frequent visits to the pub, I have noticed that this is a common view that is held by these expats, and they take every opportunity to belittle Africa and defend Europe.

In their eyes, corruption is a uniquely African phenomenon, and African leaders could learn a lot from their European compatriots. With the likes of Laurent Gbagbo and Robert Mugabe still in office, it becomes very difficult to defend the continent when such accusations are thrown around, but I couldn't help but be struck by the hypocrisy that lay behind all these sentiments. While the ANC in South Africa is undoubtedly corrupt and guilty of gross abuses of power in its seventeen years of governance so far and many other African leaders are equally guilty on this score, one need only look at Tony Blair's government and the number of scandals they got involved in to see that corruption is not unique to Africa alone and self-serving political leadership is to be found everywhere. We all know that Margaret Thatcher and the Tories were no saints either in their many years in power. If we cross the Atlantic, we have the example of Ronald Reagan and the Iran-Contra scandal, George Bush, Dick Cheney and the likes of Halliburton etc.

While I am no apologist for corrupt African leadership and am of the opinion that they should all be brought to book for abusing the power entrusted to them by the people, I also am of the opinion that European and North American political leadership is in no way better than African leadership when it comes to corruption, brutality, abuse of power, and personal enrichment. The only difference is that whilst African leaders are often guilty of brutalising their people and committing the worst atrocities against their people, European and North American leaders have mastered the art of doing the same thing to people of other continents to enrich themselves and promote their own agendas. Witness America's illegal involvement in the destabilising of the popular Sandinista government in Nicaragua in the eighties, Bush/Blair in Iraq and Afghanistan calling the murder of innocent civilians "collateral damage" whilst engaging in a war to promote the business interests of companies closely linked with them, Obama has been no different despite the deceptive oratorical skills and charisma, Putin and his brutal massacre of civilians in Chechnya and the Northern Caucasus region etc.

What the Europeans and North Americans have mastered is the art of being brutal takers in their engagement with other people and they are happy to set aside the very principles they claim to promote in doing so. They are willing to sacrifice the lives of other people if it benefits them and their people. The attitude of the Europeans and North Americans in their engagement with other people can be accurately described by the words Charles Dickens uses in his epic novel, A Tale of Two Cities when talking about the character Monseigneur, "Monseigneur had one truly noble idea of general public business, which was, to let everything go on its own way, of particular public business, Monseigneur had the other truly noble idea that it must all go his way-tend to his own power and pocket of his pleasures, general and particular, Monseigneur had the other truly noble idea that the world was made for them. The text of his order (altered from the original by only a pronoun, which is not much) ran: the earth and the fullness thereof are mine, saith Monseigneur."

This is the same attitude betrayed by these English expats at the pub and is indicative of an attitude that prevails in Europe and North America's engagement with the rest of the world. It is the attitude of people who are takers and not passive receivers and is in many ways the kind of attitude that Africa must adopt in its engagement and trade with the rest of the world in our century. For too long Africa has been a passive receiver and now it's time that we become takers. In our engagement with Asia, North America, Europe, South America, and all the other continents we need to take on the mentality of takers.

They need us much more than we need them if we just get our act together. We have all the resources they need to grow their economies and just need to grow our human capital and skills base to exploit these resources to our benefit, something we can do without outside assistance if we use all that we have at our disposal at present. We need to set the agenda for trade and if it doesn't benefit us then we refuse to engage. We need to engage at a global level on our terms and stop buying into this idea that we still need external help and support to sort ourselves out. We just need to get our act together and realise that we are in no way inferior and hence need not be dependent. This is where plans like NEPAD fell apart because they were still too dependent on outside support for success even though they claimed to promote independence and self-sufficiency.

The world belongs to those who are takers and this attitude of superiority that is being shown by these English expats at my local pub is indicative of a taker's mindset in Europe and North America's engagement with the rest of the world and needs to characterise Africa and its leadership in their engagement with the rest of the world in this century. Even the Chinese in their engagement with Africa have shown a certain superiority complex and it is important that we address this now before it becomes a problem for future generations of Africans in this century as we look to turn Africa around.

Prejudice

A couple of weeks ago I was at one of my favourite watering holes in Bryanston, Johannesburg, enjoying a few pints of Guinness with an English mate of mine who now resides in South Africa. We were sitting at the bar with another mate of his from Britain and these two Brits spent most of the time complaining about people from other cultures, basically belittling them as much as possible.

They hate the French for historical reasons that only they can articulate. They hate the "Japs" as they call them, as well as the Irish, Germans, and of course "Africans" simply because they are inferior, inadequate and can never do anything right if these Englishmen are to be believed. Whilst typically enjoying my pint of Guinness I turned around and asked them a simple question which they couldn't answer, "how can you hate people just simply because they are different from you?" It surprised me that people so well-travelled could be so narrow-minded. I have never been outside the continent of Africa, but I found my world to be much bigger than these well-travelled Brits. I found that I embraced the world much more than these people who had been all over the world and it made me realise how silly prejudice and a feeling of cultural superiority is.

Through my love of literature and the arts, I had embraced more of the world than these well-travelled, parochial Brits. A week after this event I was at my other favourite watering hole, a quaint little Irish pub in Fourways, Johannesburg and I ended up sitting next to an Afrikaner man from "die Republiek van Delmas" just outside Johannesburg and over the course of the evening I had a conversation with this man which broke all stereotypes and yet again revealed to me how foolish it is to hate people just because of the ethnic group they come from.

Firstly, we talked (as is always the case with most conversations I am involved in) politics and found that we agreed on most things and had a lot more in common than would have been obvious at first glance. Here was this Afrikaner man who fitted every stereotype, who lived on a plot in some dorpie, finding common ground with me on issues political, unheard of in South Africa. We talked about rugby and discovered not only that I knew more about rugby than this Afrikaaner man but was more passionate about the game than him, also unheard of in our country.

He was open and honest with me about the prejudices held by his community against black people, even those closest to him like his wife and yet despite all that he was completely free of the same prejudice and was able to mix with people of all types which enriched his life greatly. It then occurred to me that maybe we should spend more time at pubs drinking together. Maybe then we will truly become a nation. On a more serious note though, all of this just made me realise how shallow prejudice is and how much we miss out on by allowing ourselves to stereotype and bracket people. I exchanged cards with the Afrikaner man, and we promised to meet again in the not-too-distant future for a few dops (I love a Klippies and Coke now and then) and some decent conversation. Perhaps that is the way forward for South Africa.

The World Cup in The Light Of The African Renaissance

So there I was at the Irish pub that I frequent all too often, downing a pint of Guinness, watching the World Cup opening ceremony and like every South African, filled with pride that we had pulled it off and a sense of joyful disbelief at the fact that we were witnessing a World Cup in Africa, something which most Africans will admit we never thought we would see in our lifetime, though we secretly hoped that it would happen.

It then dawned on me that I am part of a generation of black people who have seen many walls come down, which had previously seemed insurmountable. It was Frantz Fanon who famously stated," However painful it may be for me to accept this conclusion, I am obliged to state it: for the black man there is only one destiny, and it is white." Given the context of the times in which he lived, Fanon's words could be said to represent the outlook of so many black people, whose only option in life seemed to be to try and succeed in a world that was primarily defined by the white man. Not so for this generation of black people. Significantly, the first African World Cup is taking place at the end of the first decade of the twenty-first century, a century which has begun with the hope that it could be Africa's century, that the time has finally come for the black man to take his place at the centre of world civilization. The first decade of the twenty-first century has seen a few significant walls coming down which gives us great hope that this generation of black Africans will indeed usher in an African Renaissance. We have seen Africa host its first football World Cup, we have seen a black man dominating what is traditionally a white, elitist sport (Tiger Woods in golf), we have seen two black girls dominating another sport that is traditionally white (the Williams sisters in tennis), we have witnessed Formula One's first black champion (Lewis Hamilton) and we have witnessed the historic euphoria that accompanied America's election of its first black president (Barack Obama.)

All these historic and dare I suggest epoch-defining events and accomplishments, preceding that historic moment of Africa's first football World Cup give us hope that the twenty-first century can indeed be a century that is defined and led pre-eminently by the black man as opposed to what we have seen in centuries past. Now I am aware that some will accuse me of unnecessarily racialising a beautiful moment when the entire continent stood together and when the entire world stood united behind Africa, however, I would argue that we cannot allow World Cup euphoria to distort the realities of the world we live in. It was Steve Biko who said, "Merely by describing yourself as black you have started on a road towards emancipation, you have committed yourself to fight against all forces that seek to use your blackness as a stamp that marks you out as a subservient being."

We still live in a world that is primarily white-dominated and white-defined and it will be largely the responsibility of this generation of young black people (Africans especially), who have witnessed these previously indomitable walls coming down, to take the initiative in leading and defining the world according to their pattern. To use the words of Steve Biko, "The blacks are tired of standing at the touchlines to witness a game that they should be playing. They want to do things for themselves and all by themselves."

The seminal moment in the World Cup opening ceremony for me was at the end of the American singer R. Kelly's performance when he put up his fist, with a black glove, which reminded me of the black power salute which became very popular during the sixties in the last century. Whether intentional or not, the singer's gesture served to highlight for me that this was not just about hosting a football event, it was a proud moment for the black race all over the world, it was yet more evidence that there is a Renaissance on the way which will put the black man at the forefront of human progress and development, where he rightfully belongs. It therefore becomes of primary importance that young, black Africa is aware of this seminal moment in history and seizes the day. The words of Frantz Fanon are important for us in this regard, "each generation must discover its mission, and then fulfil it or betray it in relative capacity." The walls of impossibility have come down for young black people all over the world. We have seen enough evidence through the first ten years of the twenty-first century to convince us that the black man can lead and define the world in the twenty-first century and beyond.

We must take advantage of this historically unprecedented moment for black people because as much progress as we have seen in the last decade, it is still a fact that the black man is still very much on the periphery of global leadership, influence, and development. Even the examples we have of black people who have succeeded are still quite deceptive because they are largely just examples of black people who have succeeded in a predominantly white-defined and dominated environment. We still live in a world where white competency and black incompetency are still the accepted paradigm. In South Africa, we still find ourselves in an environment where young black people go into the working world with this constant, often unspoken pressure to prove themselves because it is often assumed that they are incompetent until they prove otherwise, whereas young white South Africans go into the working world often being expected to excel until they prove otherwise and even that is something that is often covered up. So, we find that the black man is still struggling to succeed in a world which is not primarily defined by him. We witnessed this in the typical Afro-pessimism that dominated European media before the start of the World Cup as many Europeans assumed that something would naturally go wrong as the World Cup came to Africa.

So, whilst we celebrate the currently successful hosting of the first football World Cup in Africa, we need to acknowledge that at present it is nothing more than the African proving to a sceptical European audience that he can produce something of style, class, and excellence. We need to move towards a world where the African does not have to constantly feel the need to prove himself to an audience that is clearly hostile to him. This phenomenon can be likened to the experiences of the great black American, W.E.B Du Bois who famously said of his experience as a black man in a world that was hostile to him, "It is a peculiar sensation, this sense of always looking at oneself through the eyes of others, of measuring one's soul by the tape of a world that looks on in amused contempt and pity." It is a fact of life that despite some of the ground-breaking successes that black people have witnessed over the first decade of the twenty-first century, the world still looks at Africa, black people and blackness with, "amused contempt and pity" to use the words of Du Bois.

The challenge for this generation of Africans and blacks the world over is to take advantage of the current momentum and redefine and lead the world on their terms. It is not enough to be content with succeeding in a white-defined, white-dominated world. It is not enough to just be content with the freedom to define ourselves according to our terms; we need to seek to define the world and history at large on our terms. To put Africanness and blackness at the centre of world civilization. We need to be a generation of Africans and blacks, who will be empire builders, who will seize the initiative and lead and define the world in the twenty-first century and beyond. Unless we do this, we will be stuck with the current phenomenon of just merely striving to prove ourselves in a world that is predominantly hostile to and dismissive of our "blackness, our Africanness" and what we can contribute to the cause of world civilization. We will continue to perpetuate the phenomenon identified by W.EB Du Bois, "the shadow of a mighty Negro past flits through the tale of Ethiopia and of Egypt, the Sphinx. Throughout history, the powers of single blacks flash like falling stars and die somehow before the world has rightly gauged their brightness." Unless we see the successes of the likes of Obama, Woods, The Williams sisters, a successful first African World Cup etc. as an opportunity to wrestle back the initiative to define and lead the world from the white man, all we will continue to experience will be flashes of black excellence that are like falling stars in a white-dominated world, to continue with Du Bois' analogy.

To take the initiative in this regard we will need to, in the words of the French philosopher Michel Foucault, "be there at the birth of ideas, the bursting outwards of their force: not just in books expressing them, but in events manifesting this force, in struggles carried on around ideas, for or against them." This is imperative because it is ideas that shape history, that define nations, societies and historical epochs. It was Albert Camus who said that, "great nations and big empires and civilizations are often created through great ideas and dreams of men and women, for ideas do not die." Young Africa must seize this opportunity to define and lead the world by being at the forefront of the development and contestation of ideas. Young Africa must seize the opportunity to usher in an African Renaissance that will put Africa at the apex of world civilization just like the European Renaissance did for Europe. So, as we celebrate this historic moment of the first African World Cup let us be cognisant of the opportunity presented to us as Africans and blacks at the beginning of the twenty-first century. Africa must arise, carpe diem, lead, innovate, and define the world in the twenty-first century. We must take heed to W.E.B DU Bois' words, "Now is the accepted time, not tomorrow, not some more convenient season. It is today that our best work can be done and not some future day or future year. It is today that we fit ourselves for the greater usefulness of tomorrow. Today is the seedtime, now are the hours of work." Arise! Africa arise!

3

South Africa: Cry the Beloved Country

I Don't Like Black People

I read an interesting article in one of the South African papers in the last week which got me thinking about the concept of nation-building. Afrikaner author Annelie Botes said," "I don't like black people, I don't understand them. I know they are people just like me. I know they have the same rights as me. But I do not understand them. And then I do not like them. I avoid them because I am scared of them." As a black person, my natural reaction was anger and resentment at what I initially felt was a racist statement which is typical of untransformed, white South Africans. However, as I reflected further on this issue, I began to question my initial assumption and to wonder if there was anything fundamentally wrong with this statement at all.

Botes also blamed black people for South Africa's violent crime problem, which had claimed the life of her neighbour. She also alleged that violence showed that blacks were, "angry because of their own incompetence." Naturally, this statement caused a huge uproar in race-sensitive South Africa and the author was lambasted for daring to express her views. Having got past my initial angry reaction, I tried to look at this statement in the most objective manner possible and realised that there were important truths in it that we as South Africans need to acknowledge and address if we are ever truly going to attain the status of nationhood. Firstly, it dawned on me that all this woman was doing was expressing an honest opinion that she holds about black people. She wasn't singing "Kill the black man," or mouthing off slogans like "One black man, one bullet." She just simply said she does not like black people, she is afraid of black people and hence she avoids them as much as possible. She acknowledged that black people have rights just like she does. She acknowledged that black people are human beings like her, yet was very open and honest about her mistrust of black people and her fear of them.

The problem with us as South Africans is that we don't know how to get beyond emotive responses to deal with the heart of the matter when it comes to our public discourse. We would rather pretend that we are this "happy clappy" Rainbow Nation that is united until we are jolted back into reality by statements such as the one made by Annelie Botha. The truth of the matter is that race is still a big issue in South Africa, despite our denialism and our pretence of being reconciled and united. If we are ever going to successfully become a nation we must learn to be honest with each other and allow the different race groups in South Africa to express their honest opinions about members of the opposite race and to begin this honest dialogue, without allowing our emotions to cloud the issue. I am sure that it wouldn't be an exaggeration to say that the sentiments expressed by Annelie Botha reflect the views of quite a significant number of white South Africans. Many of them in their private conversations will openly admit that they fear black people, they don't like black people and that they blame black people for the crime and incompetence that characterises post-Apartheid South Africa.

To become a nation, we need to dialogue around these views, fears, and concerns. We need to tackle them and address them to understand each other better without resorting to emotive populism. Now I am not saying that we should allow people to openly promote racism and ideologies that divide and separate us. I am saying that we need a national dialogue that is open, truthful, and brutally honest if we are ever going to truly become the united "Rainbow nation" that we aspire to be. Just as black South Africans have genuine concerns, fears, and frustrations with white South Africans and the perceived lack of genuine "transformation" in the "new" South Africa, so do white South Africans have genuine concerns about black South Africans and their perceived culpability for the high levels of crime, corruption, and incompetence that have come to define the "new' South Africa. Now if you were to take off your "racial lenses" and try to look at the concerns of both races objectively, there are elements of truth in the perspectives and fears of both races about the other and the journey towards a united nationhood entails bringing these out into the public domain and addressing them in a manner that is mature and free of bias.

We black South Africans need to acknowledge (as tough a truth to swallow as it is) that most of the violent crime in this country is perpetuated by people of our race, most of the enterprises, organisations, and structures that have been started or run by black people have been characterised by high levels of corruption and incompetence. This is an inconvenient truth that black South Africans need to deal with. Now I am not saying that corruption, crime, and incompetence are the preserve of black people only, but it would be difficult to argue against the fact that these three phenomena have been most prevalent where black people have been in charge.

White South Africans need to acknowledge that from a socio-economic perspective not much has changed for the black majority in South Africa and this breeds growing and increased frustration. For all the talk by white South Africans of BEE and affirmative action affecting their job prospects in present-day South Africa, the pure economic facts are that the white majority is in a better position post-Apartheid than during Apartheid. Black South Africans resent the apparent "lack of transformation" that this reflects. White South Africans also need to acknowledge that there is a perception that they have refused to come out of their "laager" in the post-Apartheid era and have instead chosen to close ranks and live almost as a separate society. Black people feel that they have made more of an attempt to reach across and understand white South Africans whilst white South Africans have remained in their comfort zone. Whether true or not, these are some of the perceptions that South Africans across the racial divide hold and if we are truly going to be a nation they need to be addressed in an open, honest manner without the different sides taking offence and throwing out emotive responses. We need to allow the Annelie Botes of this world to openly state that they "don't like black people" without losing sight of the greater goal of building a 'Rainbow Nation."

We also need to truthfully acknowledge that we don't have to like each other to build a winning nation. We certainly have to respect each other's right to exist and to dignity, to value each other as human beings, but whoever said we have to like each other to work together towards building a winning nation? Just for the record, I also have many issues with black people just like Annelie Botes, yet that does not make me less committed to the vision of a united, prosperous South Africa any more than it does for Annelie Botes.

Workers United Against the Poor

The recent public sector strikes in South Africa, which brought the country to its knees and showcased the strength of trade unions in South Africa was a stark reminder to us all of the huge income disparity between the average South African and the educated elite as well as the conflicting class interests that constitute the make-up of post-Apartheid South Africa.

As I was following the story through various media, I was reminded of the words of Samir Amin, the Director of the Third World Forum which is based in Senegal," South Africa is a microcosm of the world system. A first world, with people with standards of living and patterns of consumption which are similar to Europeans and North Americans, and an industrialising Third World, which is a world of labour with relatively high productivity, low wages, terrible forms of oppression, exploitation in modern industries, and so on... You also have the Fourth World, which is the marginalised. It is the Bantustan; it is the suburbs with the informal settlements, unemployment, criminality, and no hope of surviving. You do not find all of this in one country. But you have all three in South Africa. Since the global picture is ugly, it is even uglier when concentrated in one country. It is an obscene society." Whilst the sentiments expressed by Amin are not new, they got me thinking about class division in South Africa and the role it played in the recent public sector strikes.

Unlike Amin, my analysis is that South Africa is not divided into three, but into four classes: the rich "capitalist" class, the middle class, the working class, and finally the unemployed poor. When the public sector strike was at its peak, what struck me to the core was that the most affected people were not the rich "capitalist" class, nor the middle class or the "striking" working class, but rather the unemployed poor. They are the ones who rely the most on state services for sustenance and survival. When the working class goes on strike to advance and promote its interests, it has the unintended consequence of affecting the poorest in society more than any other group.

It became clear to me that although COSATU and the trade unions in South Africa are often thought of as representing the poorest of the poor, in reality, they don't. They represent the 2-4 million members who make up their membership and often they promote the interests of the working/workerist class at the expense of the unemployed poor who make up the majority of South African society. In essence, we have a working class which has, whether intentionally or not is another matter, united to promote its interests at the expense of the poorest of the poor. This is a tragedy of immense proportions as the unions have posited themselves as the representatives of the poor.

In essence, it is the people in the "Fourth World" who suffered the most during the period of the public sector strike. They are the ones who rely on public hospitals, public schools, and all sorts of government services to attain a "better life." It was they and their children who were dying in state hospitals when the nurses were on strike, it is their children who are most likely going to struggle to perform academically this year because of having spent so many weeks away from school and not being able to catch up with the rising academic workload now that they are back at school.

Even the pro-worker labour policies that are advocated by the trade unions in South Africa have the unintended consequence of protecting the jobs of the working class whilst disadvantaging the unemployed poor because it makes it difficult for entrepreneurship to flourish and hence for new businesses to thrive which would mean the creation of new jobs which would absorb those who are currently unemployed and bring them into the workforce. So here again we see how labour and the unions have united (whether intentionally or not) to disadvantage the unemployed poor who are the majority in South African society or the "wretched of the earth" in the timeless words of Frantz Fanon. At an institutional level, you have forums like NEDLAC which represent business, labour, and the government, whilst leaving out the unemployed poor. So, here again, we have a structure within society that includes the three classes: the rich "capitalist" class, the middle class and the working class, whilst excluding the majority: the unemployed (and unemployable according to some crude economists).

The question is: why is no one seeing this and doing anything about it? A large percentage of these unemployed poor people are young people who are age twenty-five and under. This is a complete social disaster, which has huge ramifications for the future of this nation, yet nobody seems to care enough to push for radical social transformation. Big business is just keen to promote and advance its interests, the middle class (including the black middle class) is also focussing on advancing its interests at the expense of the workers and the poor, and the working class is also punting its sectional interests at the expense of the unemployed poor whilst pretending to represent them. The unemployed poor continue to exist on the periphery of South African society, in the informal settlements right next to wealthy suburban establishments, in the rural areas made up of the old Bantustans and self-governing territories where service delivery is poor, and quality of life is appalling. The damning reality is that it is the same working class who protest annually for wage increases and who are selling the unemployed poor short. It is the working class who deliver substandard services to the unemployed poor in government schools through teachers who are not dedicated to their learners; it is the working class who deliver substandard services to the poor in state hospitals where the quality of service given is inhumane at the best of times. It is the working class who deliver substandard services to the poor and cause blockages in service delivery at every level of public service and yet they continue to demand increases and more employment benefits each year. In short, the working class is guilty of treating the unemployed poor with contempt just like business and the middle class do. They protect their jobs at the expense of the creation of jobs that would absorb more people into employment, through their promotion of labour-friendly policies that discourage enterprise and increase labour costs.

The point is not to pick on the working class as the supreme evil in society but to highlight the fact that they are just as much the enemy of the unemployed poor as the rich "capitalist" class and the middle class are. There is no difference. South African society has united and built institutions and social structures that increasingly marginalise the poor and the workers are part of this conspiracy.

We need to build a society where the social balance of power is in favour of the subalterns. At the moment the scales are tipped against them and even those who pretend to represent them (the working class), are positioned against them to protect and promote their sectional interests. Next time you think about COSATU and the trade unions and you hear them talking about the poor and pretending to represent them, remember that it is all a farce. It is the working class who are represented by COSATU and the unions. The unemployed poor have been left out of the "social contract" of the new South Africa. Their plight is best described by the words of that great African-American intellectual, W.E.B Du Bois, "To be a poor man is hard, but to be a poor man in a land of dollars is the very bottom of hardships."

The Transformation Lie in South Africa

Last Thursday I had the opportunity to attend the annual Tomorrow's Leader Convention at the Sandton Convention Centre in Johannesburg, in my capacity as the editor of feintandmargin.com. This was an excellent conference with speakers of the highest calibre, top of which was renowned futurist and scenario planner Clem Sunter who gave an excellent presentation on South Africa and its future prospects in a world that is not only in crisis but is in the midst of radical and rapid change. Sunter was insightful, thought-provoking, and inspiring.

The complete antithesis to Sunter's presentation was a presentation given by SA Government Communications and Information Systems (GCIS) Director and SA Cabinet Spokesperson, Jimmy Manyi, on the very hot issue of transformation. Manyi gave a typically fiery presentation on the lack of genuine transformation amongst SA corporates and sought to show that very little had changed in corporate South Africa between 1994 and now and that whites still held the majority of the economic power and were refusing to let go.

Manyi's presentation was full of facts about the lack of black representation on the JSE, on the boards of most of SAs top corporates and even at various levels of management within those organisations, which I will not try to dispute as that would be a futile exercise. Manyi's solution to the current "untransformed" state of corporate South Africa and the South African economy at large was to call for more regulation by the state to enforce transformation and give blacks greater representation and control of the SA economy, more racial quotas, EE legislation, and BEE charters.

Having listened to Manyi's argument in-depth I couldn't help but notice the obvious flaw in it and as a result, I put up my hand to ask him a question which he couldn't/wouldn't answer but instead threw a cheap ad hominem argument at me which exposed the lack

84

of genuine substance in his argument. After taking in all the facts and figures which showed a need to ensure more black participation in the ownership and running of the SA economy, what struck me was that the solution that was being promoted by Manyi sought to replace white faces with black faces to engineer greater representation without in any way addressing the structural issues in the South African economy that have kept almost seventy per cent of the South African population out of the formal economy and has produced a nation with a large percentage of the population existing as nothing more than second-class, second-rate citizens despite their rights being entrenched in the constitution, which is acknowledged as one of the best in the world.

What Manyi was basically suggesting was that we remove a small, minority white elite and replace them with a small minority black elite at the helm of the South African economy and only once that is done can we say that transformation has taken place and South Africa has truly moved forward post-1994. This is a lie which needs to be debunked. Transformation is not about getting more black faces in management positions, it's not about giving blacks greater control of the JSE and most of SAs top companies. Transformation is about building an economy which allows all South Africans, whatever their background, race, ethnicity, or class to prosper if they are willing to apply themselves, show some initiative, work hard, innovate, and have the right attitude.

True transformation is about removing the barriers that have kept a large percentage of the population impoverished and living in third-world squalor whilst a minority made up of black, white, Indian, and Coloured South Africans prospers. True transformation is about removing the structural imbalances that have kept the majority of South Africans backward with no hope of ever creating a better life for themselves and their children.

We would be much better off focussing on addressing those issues as a transformation imperative rather than racial quotas which have done nothing but create an arrogant black elite which treats the poor majority no better than the white minority did under

Apartheid. I know this is not a very popular view, but I do think it is the correct view.

The narrow focus on racial quotas at the top end of the scale has allowed a minority to flourish even at the expense of the majority. The Apartheid era SA economy relied on cheap, unskilled, uneducated labour to create the conditions for an elite white minority to prosper. The post-Apartheid South African economy still relies on cheap, unskilled, uneducated labour to create the conditions for an elite minority to prosper, only this time that minority is not just made up of whites but also includes blacks, Coloureds, and Indians.

If Manyi was serious about transformation he would spend most of his time working at addressing issues such as the poor education system which keeps the majority of South Africans, who happen to be black because of a divided history, from extricating themselves from poverty and building a better, more prosperous life for themselves and their families in this much celebrated "new" South Africa.

Things Fall Apart

Alarm bells should be ringing at the events that we have witnessed over the past few weeks in South Africa. The time for passivity has passed and now is the time for ordinary South Africans to rise and take a stand, lest we go down the same route as the rest of the continent.

We have a president whose family are getting richer and richer through their political connections whilst most of the country is becoming increasingly impoverished. This means that we are fast becoming a kleptocracy, like Mobutu's Zaire where the first family is growing increasingly affluent at the expense of the rest of society.

The president's nephew, Khulubuse Zuma and Nelson Mandela's grandson, Zondwa Mandela own a company which has failed to pay its poor workers for over a year, to such an extent that one of those workers recently committed suicide after having lost everything he owned as he could not afford to pay his monthly bills, yet at the same time we see the president's nephew donating over a million rand to the ruling party and living opulently, drinking expensive champagne, smoking the finest Cuban cigars, and showing off his assortment of expensive cars. All of this is happening right before our eyes and apart from the usual complaints and moans by ordinary South Africans, no one is moved enough to take radical action.

The police shoot an innocent protestor who is part of a crowd that is protesting the lack of service delivery by the government, in scenes reminiscent of the way the Apartheid-era police force treated black people and yet again apart from the usual suspects moaning and complaining, there is no mass reaction to this shocking occurrence.

A government minister has the audacity to spend hundreds of thousands of rands of government money travelling overseas to go visit his imprisoned girlfriend under the guise of conducting official government business and yet again ordinary South Africans are surprisingly apathetic and not shocked enough to be stirred to action. This same minister is also building an expensive mansion in his rural homeland, at the taxpayer's expense, with a road being built to go past his house even though the surrounding areas are characterised by a lack of infrastructure and basic services and yet again we are surprisingly passive and not angered enough to take action.

State security agencies and the intelligence community are used in the factional battle for power within the ruling party and no one is alarmed enough to issue a call to action to the South African citizenry. All these things seem to have become so normal that it seems that we no longer get shocked as South Africans. I could go on and on because the stories are endless, but the point has been made. How did Mandela's Rainbow Nation degenerate to this level? What will it take for us to say enough is enough? I am no alarmist. I am no Afro-pessimist as some typically parochial black

Saffas may call me. I am just a concerned South African, saying enough is enough!

We need to draw the line right now before it is too late. South Africa is on the same trajectory as most post-independence African states and sadly for us that is not an upward curve. Most post-independence African states degenerated into kleptocracy and eventually became failed states because ordinary citizens ignored all the obvious signs of decay and suffered from a foolish sense of exceptionalism, and I fear that we in South Africa are guilty of the same. It is time for mass action, for "Tunisian style" protests and civil action against our government and the levels of corruption, mediocrity, conceit, and naked thuggery that are fast destroying the great potential that this nation possesses. We need "Tunisian style" protests to force the regime to change its modus operandi and improve its performance and its attitude towards its citizens; otherwise, we will be guilty of "fiddling whilst Rome burns." The time for action is now fellow South Africans. It is time to take a stand. It is time for action. May history not record the words of the Irish poet, W B Yeats as being true of contemporary South Africa, "things fall apart, the centre cannot hold.... the best lack all conviction whilst the worst are full of passionate intensity."

Ubuntu Is a Myth

A few days ago, I was sitting at a coffee shop at Montecasino in Fourways, Johannesburg with two budding South African entrepreneurs, discussing business. Whilst discussing business, we started discussing South African politics because one of the two people I was sitting with happens to have some high-level political connections which have been beneficial to him in his business endeavours.

He began to share stories of various encounters that he has had with other businessmen who have approached him hoping that he could get them an audience with certain key political figures whom he happens to know quite well so that these businessmen could advance their personal interests. What became quite apparent as we continued to talk was the fact that South Africa has reached a stage where the majority of the people will do almost anything to succeed and make money, without any consideration for ethics, morality, and the damage that could be inflicted upon society as a whole. We have become a nation of "Darwinists" who are willing to trample upon one another to achieve our goals and objectives.

The belief that black South Africans are bound by some kind of communal code called "Ubuntu" which causes them to look out for one another is a myth which needs to be debunked for the sake of the health of our nation. We have become a nation that has embraced the ethos identified by the French philosopher Michel de Montaigne, "the profit of one man is the demise of another... no profit whatever can possibly be made but at the expense of another. "The sooner we acknowledge this, the sooner we can do away with failed policies such as Affirmative Action, Black Economic Empowerment, and Employment Equity which are based on the assumption that giving a few black people greater access to economic power and opportunities will benefit the black majority, as the few who have access to opportunities will pave the way and create opportunities for others to follow. This is a pure myth and has had devastating consequences for our nation.

The reality is that there is no difference between an affluent black person and an affluent white person. Both are self-seeking, self-serving, and selfish because they are human before being black or white and human beings of whatever race share the same selfish, greedy nature. The other myth is that poor people are more altruistic than rich people. The reality is that people are human before they are rich or poor and human beings are primarily selfish and greedy. The reality is that there is no such thing as Ubuntu in South Africa anymore at every level of society. Everyone is looking out for "number one" and is willing to do anything to get ahead, even if it means destroying each other. In the words of the Ghanaian novelist Ayi Kwei Armah in his classic novel, The Beautiful Ones Are Not Yet Born, "Everybody is swimming towards what he wants. Who wants to remain on the beach asking the wind, how...how...how?"

Even those who preach morality and pretend to care about the plight of others, such as the Communists and the Unionists turn out to be nothing but hypocrites. As Oscar Wilde put it, "And what sort of lives do these people, who pose as being moral lead themselves, my dear fellow? You forget that we are in the native land of the hypocrite." For South Africans of different classes, races, and ethnicities it now appears that the "South African Dream" is to milk the system and get something for nothing and that's why we have such high levels of crime, corruption, violence, and abuse. In answer to the question posed by those two great South African entrepreneurs, John Hunt and Reg Lascaris in their must-read book, The South African Dream, "Are we grubby materialists or high idealists?" I would venture to say that the answer is clear for all to see when looking at South African society. We have long ago ceased to hold to any kind of high ideals. We are a nation of grubby materialists who don't care about one another in the final analysis.

It is time we stopped pretending to care about one another and acknowledge this truth. It is the law of the jungle that now predominates in South Africa. It is survival of the fittest at every level. The sooner we acknowledge this, the sooner we can establish and uphold institutions that will guard against the natural propensity to be selfish that every human being possesses and help us create a competitive society, based on the assumption that everyone is self-seeking, with a few checks and balances built in to ensure that this competition occurs in the fairest manner humanly possible. To assume that we still care about one another and build a society based on that assumption is to set ourselves up for failure. The evidence is all around for us to see. In South Africa, Ubuntu has gone the way of the dodo and the quagga, as in every other part of the world because of the reality of human nature.

The idealistic notions held up by the likes of Steve Biko during our Anti-Apartheid struggle as evidenced in the following words uttered by him, "we always refrain from using people as stepping stones. Instead, we are prepared to have a much slower progress to make sure that all of us are marching to the same tune", have long ago been proven to have been nothing but unrealistic, impractical theoretical notions, in contemporary South Africa. In the final analysis, Ubuntu is nothing but a myth.

The sooner we realise that our biggest problem is not race, class, or ethnicity but human nature the better we can become at constructing a winning nation. We need to throw away concepts such as Ubuntu, which are highly impractical and have no practical manifestation in contemporary South African society. Ubuntu is a myth. To paraphrase the words of a great South African and an esteemed intellectual, Dr Mamphele Ramphele, "It is hard to recognise any reflection of Ubuntu in many areas of South African society where one is confronted with abuse and greed at a junior and a senior level."

Sobukwe: Forgotten but Not Irrelevant

As I was reading the daily papers over the past week, I came across a story that reminded me of one of South Africa's finest sons, a true patriot, a genuine revolutionary, a visionary leader and an exemplary intellectual: the founding-president of the Pan Africanist Congress (PAC), Robert Mangaliso Sobukwe. The story in question was about a call by the ruling party in South Africa for more people to volunteer to ensure better delivery of services. Whilst reading that story, I came across a comment from a member of the public who said, "I wish that the politicians themselves would lead the way by volunteering first, setting the example for the public to follow."

This immediately reminded me of the words of Benjamin Pogrund, Robert Sobukwe's close friend and personal biographer, commenting on Sobukwe in his brilliant biography, How Can Man Die Better, "He asked people to do only what he himself was prepared to do." As I reflected on these words and the calibre of leader that Robert Mangaliso Sobukwe was, it struck me that the legacy of Sobukwe is almost completely forgotten in contemporary South Africa and that his life and his message still hold many valuable lessons for us today.

I have always held that South Africa's three greatest political leaders of the last century are: Anton Muziwakhe Lembede, Steven Bantu Biko, and Robert Mangaliso Sobukwe. Sadly, these three leaders are almost completely forgotten in a country that has no regard for its history and its rich legacy of leadership. Of these three Sobukwe undoubtedly stood head and shoulders above, and it saddened me that he is so little remembered in a country that he loved so deeply and sacrificed so much for. I remembered Sobukwe's own words, uttered as a young student in the 1940s, with deep sadness, "this consolation I have, however, that Africa never forgets, and these martyrs of freedom, these young and budding men and women, will be remembered and honoured when Africa comes into her own." Sadly, we have forgotten. We have forgotten to honour the immense contribution made by Robert Mangaliso Sobukwe to our liberation and the great vision that inspired so many in the darkest days of our liberation struggle.

I began to think of what Sobukwe has to say to us as contemporary South Africans committed to building a prosperous, successful nation. I decided to write a series of columns consisting of a few quotes from Sobukwe and the message that they carry for us in the here and now.

- "Take away all bitterness from us and help us to work for a country where we will all love each other, and not hate each other because hate will destroy us all." (Prayer by Sobukwe when being visited by Alex Borraine whilst at Groote Schuur hospital)

In a country where so much of the discourse seems to be overshadowed by bitterness, this is a pertinent message for us to embrace. Some in this country are still holding on to the bitterness of the past, always using that as an excuse for their current plight and refusing to work together towards a better South Africa with those whom they perceive as their past oppressors. Sobukwe says to those people, 'It's time to move on, get over your bitterness from the past and work towards a better South Africa for all." Some in South Africa are bitter over the post-94 policies that have been employed by the government to redress the imbalances of the past and use that as an excuse for their current plight and lack of progress. Sobukwe says to these people, time to get over your bitterness and come up with creative and constructive ways of redressing the imbalances of the past instead of just moaning and complaining without bringing to the fore any viable alternatives.

- "A doctrine of hate can never take people anywhere. It is too exacting. It warps the mind. That is why we preach the doctrine of love, love for Africa. We can never do enough for Africa, nor can we love her enough. The more we do for her, the more we wish to do. I am sure that I am speaking for the whole of young Africa when I say that we are prepared to work with any man who is fighting for the liberation of Africa within our lifetime."

"I wish to make it clear again that we are anti-nobody, we are pro-Africa. We breathe, we dream, and we live in Africa because Africa and humanity are inseparable. It is only by doing the same that the minorities in this land, the European, Coloured, and Indian can secure mental and spiritual freedom."

In a country that is prone to polarisation of all sorts, Sobukwe's message is critical. For a country that is wrought with xenophobia, it is important to remember Sobukwe's Pan-Africanism. Our liberation struggle was not just about political and economic liberation for South Africa alone. It was a Pan-African struggle. It was driven by a love for Africa. It was motivated by a desire to see Africa as a whole advance and progress. It was inclusive of all people who loved Africa and were committed to its political and economic emancipation. There was no place for xenophobia in this Pan-Africanist vision. It was the vision that united Sobukwe. Lembede, Kwame Nkrumah, Sekou Toure, Nnamdi Azikiwe and a host of other liberation-era African leaders. It was a common vision for the whole continent. This is the vision that contemporary South Africa needs to embrace. It is time we moved away from polarisation and moved towards inclusiveness. It's time that we also had a passion for Africa as a whole and for African developmental issues. Pan-Africanism was a vision that drove Sobukwe and his ilk to self-sacrifice and service. For contemporary South Africa where the majority is more concerned with what can be done for them instead of what they can do for their country, Sobukwe has something important to say. It is about what we do for South Africa, for Africa, not just about what can be done for us. It is not just about what we can take from Africa, it is about what we can give to Africa, and what we have to offer.

- "Let me plead with you, lovers of my Africa, to carry with you into the world the vision of a new Africa, an Africa reborn, an Africa rejuvenated, an Africa re-created, young Africa. We are the first glimmers of a new dawn." (speech at the Fort Hare Completer's Social in 1949)

"The wheel of progress revolves relentlessly, and all the nations of the world take their turn at the field-glass of human destiny. Africa will not retreat! Africa will not compromise! Africa will not relent! Africa will not equivocate! And she will be heard! Remember Africa!"

In a nation and a continent that is often filled with negative stories of violence, poverty, disease, devastation, and destruction, Sobukwe has an important message to relay. It is time for us to have a new vision, to go beyond just looking at our current reality (without shifting into denialism of course) and to paint a picture of a new, transformed Africa. It is time for us as South African and African citizens to embrace this picture, this vision of a new, developed, modernised Africa and to actively play our part in bringing it to pass. It is time to get beyond all the negativism and to embrace a positive vision for Africa. If a young man like Sobukwe, living under an oppressive system like Apartheid, with limited opportunities, could find it within himself to embrace a positive vision for Africa despite adverse circumstances, how much more

94

should we do the same in a new, democratic South Africa? We have more opportunities than he did and more freedoms than he enjoyed. We thus have no reason for being pessimists when he could find it within himself to be optimistic despite his adverse reality. We can paint a picture of a new Africa and we can all work towards it.

- "I believe it was God's will that I should come here to realise how much love there is in the world and to get my sense of values right. Above all else, I have had a chance to know myself - neither saint nor devil: just a bundle of capabilities in the hands of God." (Sobukwe on 20 November 1963 talking about life in prison)

In a nation and a continent where people often blame adverse circumstances and an uncooperative environment for their negative attitudes and inability to be better people and hence better citizens, Sobukwe has a message for us from his prison cell on Robben Island where he suffered more than the other prisoners. The message is that we can all commit to growing and becoming better citizens irrespective of our external circumstances. As a wise man once said, "Your circumstances are as responsible for your character as a mirror is for your looks."

Sobukwe also reminds us as Africans, where the tendency is to deify our leaders, that they are not some mythical figures who can solve all our problems and bring to pass all our dreams. They are just ordinary, fallible human beings who have committed to making a difference. They are not more saintly or more evil than any of us. This perspective should affect our ordering and structuring of society to keep them as accountable as possible instead of treating them as gods who are the answer to all our prayers.

- "You have seen by now what education means to us: the identification of ourselves with the masses. Education to us means service to Africa. You have a mission; we all have a mission. A nation to build we have, a God to glorify, and a contribution clear to make towards the blessing of mankind. We must be the embodiment of our people's aspirations. And all we are required to do is to show the light and the masses will follow."

In a nation and a continent where education often separates the elite from the masses, where the uneducated and illiterate are often treated with contempt, where education is often used as a stepping-stone to pursuing a life of personal enrichment, wealth accumulation, and manipulation of opportunities to promote self-advancement at the expense of society at large, Sobukwe has a relevant message to share with us. Education for Sobukwe and his generation was not something that was used to arrogantly separate themselves from the masses, but rather to identify with them and their struggles. It was a responsibility to take what they had learnt and to use it not just for self-enrichment, but to uplift and serve the poor, the marginalised and the oppressed. Education was a tool to be used in the pursuit of justice for all, not just for the elite. Sobukwe also reminds us that because of its immense problems, Africa is our mission field and not just our minefield to make money. He reminds us that we all have a role to play in the development and advancement of Africa and that those who have been privileged enough to get educated have a responsibility to point the way forward for those who have not, instead of just living opulently, treating them contemptuously and not caring about their plight. He reminds us that instead of retreating into their comfortable, middle-class, suburban lifestyles, the educated elite has a duty to work towards the upliftment of the impoverished majority, that education is not just a tool to increase our capacity to earn more, but rather to increase our capacity to serve better and give more.

The life and message of Robert Mangaliso Sobukwe have so much meaning for us as South Africans as we strive to build a prosperous, successful, winning nation, and we ignore him to our peril. We need to rediscover the significance of his life and message if we are going to truly attain all the goals and objectives that we aspire to as a nation.

Sobukwe: Whites Are African Too

So, over the past weekend, I went on a road trip with three mates of mine. We drove down to Mpumalanga for a "boys' weekend" away and throughout the trip we talked a lot about pertinent issues such as race relations in South Africa, the lack of economic progress of a majority of black South Africans in a new, democratic South Africa and other such issues. As is typical in South Africa the issue of race cropped up in almost every discussion we had (of course this was amplified by the openly racist treatment we received from Blue Bull rugby fans, who are mostly Afrikaners, at Mbombela Stadium on Friday evening whilst we were watching the Bulls play the Mpumalanga Pumas.)

What intrigued me was that we were a group of four young South Africans who all went to integrated schools, have had access to quality education and opportunities and yet amid all of that we still found race and the unequal distribution of wealth along racial lines in South Africa, as a big generational challenge. This reminded me again of the importance of embracing the ideals, values, and principles that Robert Mangaliso Sobukwe stood for and provides the perfect platform for this week's column on the meaning and the message of the life of Robert Mangaliso Sobukwe to contemporary South Africa.

- "Politically we stand for the government of the Africans for the Africans by the Africans with everybody who owes his only loyalty to Africa and accepts the democratic rule of an African majority, being regarded as an African. We guarantee no minority rights because we are fighting precisely that group exclusiveness that those who plead for minority rights would like to perpetuate. It is our view that if we have guaranteed individual liberties, we have given the highest guarantee necessary and possible. I have said before, and I will still say so now, that I see no reason why, in a free, democratic Africa, a predominantly black electorate should not return a white man to parliament, for colour will count for nothing in a free Africa."

- "I know I have been accused of being anti-white, not only by the government but also by others. But there is not one who can quote any statement of mine that bears that out. When I say 'Africa for Africans' I have always made clear that by African I mean those, of any colour, who accept Africa as their home. Colour does not mean anything to me."

The sentiments expressed by Sobukwe in the above quotes pose a challenge to all South Africans. To black South Africans, the challenge is to have a more inclusive definition and understanding of Africanness. Black South Africans need to embrace those of European descent who have been on this continent for generations, who consider this continent their home and who have a rich history on this continent, as fellow Africans.

White South Africans need to ensure that their primary loyalty is to Africa and African peoples, with a clear commitment to doing everything that is within their power to make Africa successful and prosperous instead of just retreating to their "Laager" and being critical without being willing to contribute anything constructive to the growth and development of the continent. Both black and white South Africans need to find their primary identity in their South Africanness and not in their race and ethnicity. This is what it means to be a nation.

Both black and white South Africans need to learn to vote for political candidates based on their ideological outlook, their competency, and their ability to produce results, instead of the colour of their skin. With this kind of attitude, it would be easy for a black majority to vote a white leader into power because skin colour wouldn't be the determining factor, only ability and efficiency. These are the kinds of challenges that Sobukwe poses to us as contemporary South Africans.

- "My instructions, therefore, are that our people must be

taught now and continuously that in this campaign we are going to observe absolute non-violence." (From a letter distributed by the PAC, written by Sobukwe advocating non-violent resistance to the Pass laws, before the Sharpeville massacre.)

With the culture of violent protest that is prevalent in contemporary South Africa as evidenced by the recent lawless, violent strikes by trade union members, we must heed these words from Sobukwe. Our people need to be constantly and continuously taught the principle of standing up for their rights in a non-violent, non-aggressive, non-threatening manner. We must inculcate amongst our people a culture of non-violence lest we destroy ourselves under the guise of defending and promoting our individual and group rights as laid out in our constitution.

- "The old order is changing, ushering in a new order. The great revolution has started, and Africa is the field of operation... We have made our choice and we have chosen African Nationalism because of its deep human significance; because of its inevitability and necessity to world progress. World civilization will not be complete until the African has made his full contribution. Even as the dying so-called Roman civilization received new life from the barbarians, so also will the decaying so-called western civilization found a new and purer life from Africa."

These words from Sobukwe, uttered over half a century ago are still relevant, not just to us as contemporary South Africans, but to all Africans. The world is changing right before our eyes, with massive realignment in the global geo-political sphere, as countries from the developing world are stepping to the fore and banding together to have a greater say on world issues, and we as Africans must seize the opportunity afforded in this. With Africa being a key player in terms of its abundance of natural resources and China, India, the United States, and Brazil increasingly looking to the continent to meet their growing demand, Africa must take the lead and begin to set the terms with regard to trade and economic relations instead of just being dictated to. With a growing and increasingly affluent African middle class providing a huge market for global goods, the onus is on us as Africans to leverage this to our advantage. As stated by Sobukwe, "world civilization will not be complete until the African has made his full contribution." Never has this been more pertinent than in the current times. It is time for Africa to make its contribution to the cause of world progress and to lead the way.

I hope that the Sobukwe "series" has inspired you to be a better African citizen, to take steps to make your contribution to the development of Africa and to read up more on the life of one of Africa's finest leaders ever: Robert Mangaliso Sobukwe. If you are inspired to read up more on the life of Sobukwe, I encourage you to get yourself a copy of his brilliant biography, How Can Man Die Better written by his personal friend Benjamin Pogrund.

I end off with words from a speech given by Benjamin Pogrund at Sobukwe's very emotional funeral, "And we have from Bob Sobukwe that belief in South Africa of which I spoke earlier. One united South Africa, free of colour or tribal divisions. A South Africa devoted to justice and democracy for all its people, without totalitarianism, communism, or any other crushing of the human spirit. It was a dream in his lifetime; yet it is more than a dream for in it lies the future and the salvation of all of us. In all the years of his life, Bob Sobukwe did not deviate a fraction from his belief and always he wanted it to come about in peace. Going closely with this, what we have from him is a love of people." Aluta continua!

Reality Check

Watching the sudden wave of patriotism that consumed the nation just before the World Cup and seeing Bafana Bafana huff and puff their way to a historically embarrassing first-round exit at the World Cup brought to mind a few home truths about this country that are at once uncomfortable.

At the commencement of the World Cup amidst all the euphoria, the "patriots" had us all believing that South Africa was good enough to get into the knockout stages of the tournament based on their pre-tournament performances against a bunch of opponents who were in reality no-hopers and had been hand-picked for the simple purpose of building the team's and the nation's confidence and not because of their footballing ability. In other words, our expectations going into the tournament had become so distorted that they had deviated completely from reality. Anyone who dared state that Bafana was not good enough to get past the group stage was immediately accused of being "unpatriotic" even though this was a solid viewpoint based on factual evidence.

It was Malcolm X who said, "You're not supposed to be so blind with patriotism that you can't face reality." Many of us were so blinded by "patriotism" that we refused to face reality, and this seems to be a phenomenon that runs across South African society at all levels. As a nation, we seem to have a skewed perception of our position not just in Africa but on the world stage. Just like Bafana, the simple truth remains that despite its immense potential South Africa remains an average country which is underachieving due to a culture of mediocrity, blame-shifting, fanaticism, and lack of personal leadership.

In the words of Albert Camus, "Nobody realises that some people expend tremendous energy merely to be normal. "We are a nation that seems to revel in expending a lot of energy merely to produce average results. Just like Bafana who spent so much time and money on pre-world cup training camps in Europe and at home only to produce average results at the tournament, South African society is filled with many examples of tremendous energy being expended only to produce average results. That is why for example we are spending increased amounts of money, effort etc. every year on education and yet the results don't seem to be getting any better, if anything they are getting worse. The reason for this is that despite all the money being spent, our teachers are average, education department officials are average, pupils and learners in schools have an average work ethic and commitment to education and hence produce average results etc.

We are not a society that is given to excellence and being exceptional. We are too content with mediocre results. We are a mediocre society and as much as this is an inconvenient truth, our current mediocre political leadership is merely an accurate reflection of the society that we live in. As the poet W.H. Auden said, "All that we are not stares back at what we are." We are not as exceptional as we think we are. In many ways, the miracle of the negotiated transition that brought an end to Apartheid and the international acclaim that came with that as well as the fact that we were in the fortunate position of having a global statesman like Nelson Mandela, has fostered this false sense of exceptionalism amongst South Africans which needs to be nipped in the bud if we are indeed going to fulfil our potential as a nation and become the global force that we aspire to be.

The fact of the matter is that even when measured against other developing countries who are in the same place as us, such as the BRIC countries (Brazil, Russia, India, and China) South Africa still lags behind in a manner that should be alarming to all of us who want to see this country maximise its potential and become the global powerhouse that it can potentially be. This requires that we become a society that takes an honest look at ourselves in the mirror and embraces a few tough truths, as Simone de Beauvoir said, "I tore myself away from the safe comfort of certainties through my love for truth-and truth rewarded me." Just like Bafana at the World Cup, we need a reality check of our current status and position on a global scale.

An important lesson we can learn from the Bafana story is that it does not help to bring in experts who are at the top of their field (e.g.Carlos Alberto Parreira, Carlos Queiroz etc) if there is no underlying work ethic and quality to undergird that. The best these experts can do is to paper over a few cracks and provide a few short-term, quick fixes but they can't solve the structural problems that need to be addressed to make us competitive on a global level.

Just like with Bafana, if the players are average and the coach is excellent, there is only so far he can take them. If we as a society continue to embrace, tolerate, and in some instances celebrate mediocrity, then we can only go so far as a nation. It is time that we push ourselves to greater levels of excellence and achievement as a nation. Let us put an end to this mediocrity. Just as we have seen mass protests by workers demanding higher wages over the last year and a half, let us see ourselves protesting all mediocrity in our nation. Let us protest for higher productivity levels amongst our workers, greater levels of excellence and a better work ethic from our teachers, higher commitment levels and greater work ethic amongst our learners and pupils etc. These are the kinds of things that we will need to stand up for if we are to see South Africa taking its rightful place amongst the nations of the world in the twenty-first century.

Lessons For SA From Egypt's "People's" Revolution

The popular revolution in Egypt which led to the ousting of President Hosni Mubarak duly reminded me of the words uttered by the American poet Walt Whitman, "A great city (nation-state) is that which has the greatest men and women." The orderly, disciplined, and principled manner in which ordinary Egyptians protested against a stubborn tyrannical government until they got the result they wanted holds many lessons for contemporary South Africa.

For the political leadership of South Africa, the primary lesson to be learnt is that leaders need to listen to the people they lead and be prompted to respond to their grievances. Leaders need to stop taking the people for granted and rather respect and serve them. We must remind ourselves that the "Egyptian revolution" began primarily not as a call for political change but rather as a revolt against economic hardship. Whilst the leadership of the country were living in the lap of luxury, the average Egyptian was struggling to make ends meet and just barely getting by. This is a phenomenon that you find prevalent in South Africa. Whilst the elite are living in the lap of luxury, the majority have sub-standard living conditions, poor economic prospects, and very little hope of creating a better life for themselves.

This is a state of affairs which is not sustainable and needs urgent attention instead of the lip service that the current political leadership is paying to it. The grievances of ordinary citizens can be ignored for only so long before the people revolt and overthrow the current government and political and social system. For ordinary South Africans the primary lesson to be learnt from the "Egyptian revolution" is that there is a way of protesting, expressing our grievances and trying to bring about change which is non-violent, civil, and orderly. Too often our civil protests are violent, disorderly, and lacking in civility. As Frantz Fanon said, "There is a point at which our methods devour themselves." Because of the violent and aggressive nature of our struggle against Apartheid, it seems that we have become incapable of expressing our dissatisfaction at the inefficiencies of our government and our political leadership in a respectable manner. We saw ordinary Egyptians keeping their streets clean, resisting the temptation to be unruly and violent despite the best attempts of the Mubarak regime to provoke them, we saw them forming a human chain around the museum in Cairo which carries so many artefacts that are central to Egyptian and human history. This showed a certain sense of national pride and civility amongst the Egyptian protesters, something sadly lacking in South Africa. Our protests often degenerate into chaos, destruction, vandalising of property, and general disorder. We can learn a lot from the "Egyptian revolution."

Another lesson that we can learn from Egyptians is what has been termed "generational mix." Whilst the "Egyptian revolution" was multi-generational in its composition and leadership, there can be no doubt that it was initiated and primarily driven by young Egyptians. It was the young people who organised, planned, and led the protests on the street. The older generation got behind them and worked with them, without in any way patronising them. The key drivers of change in Egypt were the young people. This is an important lesson not just for South Africa but for the continent. Too often it is the elderly Africans who are at the centre of the drive for change on the continent and as a result, we see very little of that happening, despite the many conferences and seminars that are held on this topic. It is the youth who can bring a fresh perspective, fresh impetus and new energy to the quest for change on the continent. It's time for the elderly generation to let the young people be at the forefront of the drive for change. This is the only way we are going to see progress on the continent.

It was quite significant to see how out of touch Hosni Mubarak and his elderly NDP leadership were with the young people of Egypt. It was almost like they spoke a different language to that spoken by the youth. Every time they communicated, they showed a lack of understanding of the dynamics of the changed political environment they were in. In South Africa, the political language and outlook of the ruling party leadership is clearly out of touch with that of ordinary South Africans, consisting mainly of young people. The same thing can be seen right through the continent. The time for young people to take over leadership and drive the agenda of the continent has come. The older generation has had its chance and they have only managed to take us so far. It's time they stepped aside and let the young people lead. Of course, they will still have a key mentorship and advisory role to play and cannot be simply discarded but what the Egyptian revolution teaches us is that it is only when young people are allowed to lead that genuine change becomes a reality.

A great example of this is the role that the young ANC Youth League leadership of Nelson Mandela, OR Tambo, Anton Lembede, AP Mda etc. played in changing the strategy and tactics of the ANC in their fight against the Apartheid regime in South Africa. Until then, the ANC had followed a certain strategy which had borne no fruit after many decades of struggle and the elderly ANC leadership at that time was set on continuing with that failed strategy. This young generation of leaders imposed their strategy on the elderly ANC leadership at the time and it is no surprise that they became the generation that brought us political emancipation in South Africa. It simply proves the point that it is when the youth are at the forefront that real change becomes possible. Another great contemporary example is Barack Obama's successful presidential campaign in 2008 which was largely dependent on an enthused and passionate young electorate which rose out of the political doldrums to put Obama into the Oval Office.

After the euphoria of the "Egyptian revolution" and its successful removal of President Hosni Mubarak has died down, what will be important to note are the lessons that can be learnt from this inspirational revolution and how those lessons can be harnessed to make South Africa and Africa better for all its citizens.

Elections Make No Difference Anyway

I want to take you on a journey this week. A journey into a large community in the northern parts of Johannesburg, South Africa, called Diepsloot. This place reflects South Africa, the old and the new. It reflects the living conditions of the majority of South Africans who live in third-world squalor whilst an elite minority enjoy comfortable, first-world living conditions. It presents a microcosmic view of all that is wrong and pitiful about South Africa, old and new. It gives first-hand evidence of the oft-stated claim that very little has changed in the new South Africa for the majority. It reveals quite plainly the utter uselessness and insignificance of democracy and elections when the majority of the voters have nothing to gain from the outcome, which is the case in contemporary South Africa.

It is election season in South Africa, local government elections are upon us. This is a time when politicians who have been ignoring the majority of citizens for the better part of their term of office suddenly discover the importance of reconnecting with the people and are seen mixing with the community, promising much to guarantee another term in office. This is what is happening in Diepsloot at present. Diepsloot is an informal settlement in northern Johannesburg, separated by a massive fence and a big sewage pipe from one of the wealthiest golfing estates in South Africa, Dainfern Ridge. It reflects the South Africa we live in. Whilst the houses on the golfing estate in Dainfern are huge and spacious, the one-roomed "RDP" houses and shacks in Diepsloot are small and overcrowded. Whilst the rich who live in Dainfern, just a five-minute distance away drive to work in expensive, luxury cars that are almost always only inhabited by one person, the poor who live in Diepsloot have to wake up early every day, walk to the "taxi rank" and queue to be driven to work in over-crowded minibus taxis by rude, unruly, and disrespectful taxi drivers.

In Diepsloot there are over a million people from all over South Africa and Africa, living in abject poverty. In Dainfern there are possibly, at most a few hundred people living in first-world luxury and comfort, separated from the poor by a fence and a sewage pipe. In Diepsloot the lights go out all the time in the evenings, whilst just across the fence you can see Dainfern glowing with light. In Diepsloot the people often go without running water or electricity for periods of up to a week at times whilst the spacious golfing estate next door is watered by massive pumps and the rich enjoy Eskom's finest service. There are almost no streetlights in Diepsloot so it is completely dark at night, whilst Dainfern is always lit up.

The statisticians tell us that the known rate of HIV/AIDS in Diepsloot is three out of five and it is almost certainly higher than that in reality. On any given day you can drive around Diepsloot and you'll find hundreds of thousands of young people sitting around with nothing to do. They are uneducated, most are illiterate, "unskilled" and unemployed (unemployable according to some economists). Over seventy per cent of this Diepsloot population is made up of young people, mostly under twenty-five years of age. Whilst the rich in Dainfern are completely walled in and have twenty-four-hour security which protects them from crime to some extent, crime levels are high in Diepsloot and life is so cheap that people stab each other fighting for as little as two rand.

The children of the rich in Dainfern go to elite schools and enjoy the best facilities and excellent teaching from their highly skilled teachers. The schools in Diepsloot are shambolic, to say the least, with pathetic facilities and teachers who are not only unskilled but are unbelievably lazy. The conditions are so poor in these schools that you get grade tens and grade elevens who can't even read, and you find yourself wondering how they even got to that level in the first place. As a result of all this you find a lot of young people who have given up on the hope of ever getting an education and instead spend most of their time drinking outrageous amounts of alcohol and engaging in promiscuity and dangerous, risky sexual behaviour that is costing South Africa hundreds of thousands of young lives if not millions. In Diepsloot the average young girl is either pregnant or already a mother to two or three kids, all dependant on government grants for their sustenance since mom is often not working and the young lad who impregnated mom is too busy having fun and being young to care for the children he helped bring into this earth.

In Diepsloot the people entertain themselves by spending their hard-earned money, which is a pittance, on alcohol and soft drugs like dagga, whilst the rich in Dainfern are dining out at fancy restaurants, going to the theatre, and doing all those things that make rich people's lives fuller than the poor. I wish to God that the place I was describing was a made-up place which didn't exist, but everything I have described is true (and probably worse than I have been able to describe it with my limited vocabulary). Diepsloot is an actual place that exists and which I worked in for two years in my quest to change the world and help build a South Africa that was more just and fair and offered a better life for all its citizens.

It is a place I cried over for many days in my two-year working stint after moving to Johannesburg from Cape Town. I would sit with young people who were in the most dire circumstances and my heart would break over them and the difficult life that awaited them, almost daily. Diepsloot is run by local Councillors who come from the ruling African National Congress, the so-called "party of the people." These Councillors have done nothing for this poor community throughout their term and are often nowhere to be found when the community is dealing with its day-to-day challenges just to survive and yet now that it is election time you see these Councillors and their seniors from the African National Congress coming into the community, pretending to be surprised by the shocking conditions in which the people live and making more empty promises to change things around if they are given another term in office.

Of course, everyone knows that this is all just empty talk and nothing much will change once the election season is over because the truth is that the ANC has long ago deviated from its stated aim of being the party that represents the interests of the majority of South Africans and has betrayed the revolutionary ideals on which it was founded even though it maintains the slogans and the songs which promise a "better life" for all South Africans if they vote ANC. Diepsloot represents the reality of a South Africa that is mostly run by an ANC government, which has become so focused on enriching an elite few that it has long ago ceased to be the revolutionary party that it claims to be. Diepsloot represents a clear picture of the way the ANC has failed the majority of South Africans most devastatingly.

Of course, the simple solution would be to encourage the people in Diepsloot to vote differently, to find a different alternative but even this would be of no help. This is so because the official opposition in South Africa, the Democratic Alliance or the Dompas Alliance as I call them have clearly shown their open contempt for the poor in the one province in South Africa which they run, the Western Cape.

Despite the DA claiming to have an excellent service delivery record and the fact that they are always telling us how excellently the Western Cape is run, the truth of the matter is that the excellent services that the DA claims to offer, are only enjoyed by its elite, minority constituency in the Western Cape and not by the poor majority. The only people who brag about how well Cape Town and the Western Cape are run, are those who are living in suburbia, enjoying a first-world lifestyle. For the poor who live in the Western Cape, there is no difference between them and the rest of the poor in South Africa who live in ANC-run territory because despite its best pretensions the DA, like the ANC is a party of the elite and only cares about reaching out to the poor who live in places like Diepsloot when it comes to election time to get votes. In the final analysis, the DA, the ANC, and all the other political parties in South Africa offer the poor who live in places like Diepsloot nothing at all and hence it leaves one feeling that elections do not make a difference anyway. They are just a terrain for elite interests to be contested at the expense of the poor, at least in South Africa that is. Most South Africans are like the character Jack Linden in Robert Tressell's novel, The Ragged Trousered Philanthropists, of whom it is said, "his life had been passed amid a civilisation which he had never been permitted to enjoy the benefits of" and for this majority of South Africans it makes no difference who is in power as the evidence has shown, so one can only conclude that elections make no difference anyway.

Reflections Of an Ordinary South African

It is a gorgeous Spring Day in Johannesburg. I am sitting at my desk doing some work. As usual, I am juggling my pastoral responsibilities and trying to keep up to date with my studies. On this day, I am reading my African Philosophy textbook and making notes. I am engrossed in an intense article on the philosophy of Negritude and its relevance to present-day Francophone African philosophical endeavours. I am grappling with the writings of the likes of Cesaire, Senghor, and Frantz Fanon.

A young man walks into our church building and takes a seat right next to my desk where I am working. His name is Macson. He is from Malawi. He came to South Africa looking for a better life, and more opportunities. Yet here he is sitting next to me looking tired and worn out. Only a week ago he and a mate of his called Sylvester had walked in on me, whilst I was doing a microeconomics assignment.

"Pastor, please pray for us. We are in desperate need of employment. We have tried every avenue. We have been waking up every day to look for work and so far, nothing has opened up for us. We are tired of sitting around with nothing to do." I look at these two young men, both from Malawi, who came to South Africa with a hope for a better life. They are not your stereotypical lazy, lethargic poor person with an entitlement mentality. They genuinely want to work. They are willing to do anything just so they can have enough money to put food on the table. I turn around and encourage them not to give up, not to throw in the towel. All it takes for things to turn around in life is just one moment, one breakthrough, and one person believing in you, one door opening. Yet what do I know? From the comfort of my desk, with plans for a future in academia and in politics, how much can I identify with these people? I promise them that I will pray for them, and they duly get up, smile and promise to come back to me with a report on their progress in finding a job.

So here sits Macson in front of me, a week after this encounter, ready to give an update on his employment status. I asked him why he wasn't at church this past Sunday. He tells me he and his mate were out "marketing" for a job on Sunday morning so he couldn't come to church. "Marketing" means a group of men, sitting on the side of the road at a particular spot where bakkies frequently come through to pick up a few guys for some kind of casual, manual labour. "Piece jobs" they call it. There are literally tens, if not hundreds of thousands of men and women who are living like this in Diepsloot. This is a way of life for them. They are not educated. They are not "skilled". They are in Fanon's famous words the" wretched of the earth."

I look at Macson. I asked him if he had any success finding a "piece" job on Sunday. He says a few other men were picked up for these odd jobs, but he and his mate Sylvester had no luck. No one picked them up. Being in a philosophical state I begin to ask myself many questions. What kind of world is it that accepts the plight of Macson and millions of others as normal? What kind of God creates a world where billions of people are stuck in a life of survival, just trying to get by? What kind of lives are we living where things like these no longer move us? Only a few days back I had been to a wedding at the Westcliff Hotel where a mate of mine and his sweetheart were getting married. The food was sumptuous, the wine was flowing. The conversation was about recent business trips to Europe. The women were all commenting on the beauty of the groom's speech, his touching, moving speech quoting Yeats et al. The best man gave a grand speech quoting Shakespeare. The couple was about to leave for Thailand the next day to go on honeymoon. Everything was pure bliss. We ate, we drank, we talked about the markets, we laughed, we danced, and we wondered who would be next in line for marriage.

Could there be two more different worlds? Is this what it means to live in a liberated South Africa? Of course, it dawns on me that all these questions and all this philosophising is of no help to Macson. He needs a job, not my socio-economic reflections. I remember the millions of conversations that I have had with my middle-class friends in the comfort of their lounges or a restaurant, of course over a glass of wine, on the poverty problem facing South Africa. I realise how easy it is to theorise and philosophise and how difficult it is to be on the front line, faced with immediate need and increasing desperation. Can we ever change the status quo? Whilst the minority spend holidays in Europe and spend weekends drinking whisky and smoking Cuban cigars, the majority struggle along, trying to make ends meet. Has anything changed really except the fact that we have a smaller group of a darker colour who can enjoy the benefits of "liberated" South Africa? Was it realistic to expect anything to change at all given the lessons of history? What is freedom anyway?

Can people be said to be free when they have to sell their souls to get money? Is there any freedom in being free to go wherever you want and to pursue whatever career you want, as long as you have the money to do so? What about the millions who don't? Where is their freedom? Surely a country with millions of Macsons, both South African-born and from outside the country, cannot claim to be truly free?

I look at Macson sitting next to me, totally oblivious to all that is happening inside my head. I give him the numbers of someone I know who may be able to help him get some kind of job. He smiles at me, gets up, and thanks me for the help I am giving him. I smile back aware that there is no guarantee that my contact will be able to help him out. Even if that happens, what about the hundreds of thousands of Macsons who are living in Diepsloot who have no one to help them yet are willing to work? The experts often accuse them of being lazy; policies are often drawn to address their plight. Conferences are held in their honour: concepts developed to discuss their condition: Sustainable development, Live Aid, Make-poverty-history, Millennium Development Goals, Summits, and academic papers. None of this has a direct bearing on the Macsons of this world.

Macson says his goodbyes and leaves me to my philosophising. I decide to put aside my philosophy readings for now and to reflect further on these issues. Of course, I have been through this whole process before. Daily, we get people walking into our church building, desperate for employment, for any job just so they can make a living. Of course, the economic analysts and the intellectual elites have some "understanding" of this. They talk about recessions, interest rate cuts, and growth rates. This is their understanding of the plight of the Macsons of this world.

I begin to wonder if this is what our celebrated heroes fought for all these years: A country like every other, with elites living in the lap of luxury whilst the majority await their salvation. I wonder why people place so much trust in other individuals to deliver them in any case. It makes no sense to me. How can the world I live in be content to punt the merits of an economic system which has left so many destitute, which has made objects out of people? Of course, the fact that the proposed alternative had suffered such a spectacular failure will be thrown to me as evidence that this system is currently the best, yet the evidence of human misery and casualisation of labour speaks a different message to me.

It is a strange country we live in. Opulence mixed with dire poverty. Of course, this is not a new thought. You don't have to be academically inclined to see this vast discrepancy. Can the gap between the Macsons of this world and those who are "living it up" ever be closed? Is it reasonable to expect this gap to be closed? All these questions bother me but what frustrates me even more is the fact that I don't have the answers. Maybe Darwin was right: it is all about the fittest surviving. This would certainly explain to me the kind of world we are in at the moment. The poor are nowhere. They rarely, if ever, receive any justice. They are on the periphery of society. Decisions are taken on their behalf without any consultation. The world runs and leaves them still ambling along. Of course, in all of this, I am not glorifying the poor. There is nothing noble and upright about poor people either. They are just as greedy, self-centred, and selfish as the wealthy. They also love money and will do anything for it, just like the rich. Yet none of this can justify the kind of conditions that we have accepted as normal for most South Africans to live in.

I am struggling to make sense of a world where there are billions of Macsons, living from hand to mouth, battling every day just to make ends meet. Where is the sense in all this? All our learning, all our enterprise, all our discussion papers and documents, all our academic pursuits and conferences have produced a world that is more unequal now than it has ever been. Every attempt to change the status quo throughout history has failed spectacularly. Religion hasn't been able to solve the problem. Politics hasn't fared any better. It begs the question why? Why all the endeavour? Why all the false hope? I was just wondering.

A country full of migrant labourers. A continent full of Macsons. Men and women for whom life holds no pleasures except for blood, sweat, and toil. What was it all about anyway, this highly celebrated liberation? It wasn't as grand as we all expected. Will the "wretched" of the earth ever have any respite? Are these questions of any benefit to the Macsons of this world? I was just wondering. In an age where hope is highly celebrated, and opportunity is scarcely created what future is there for Macson and his ilk? I wish I knew where all these questions are leading. I wish there was something I could do for every Macson of this world. We know there are many in all corners of the world, especially Asia, Latin America, Eastern Europe, and Africa. We know all this yet seem incapable of doing anything about it. I have looked to history for some semblance of hope and yet even there I found no reference point.

We live in a world that has little if any regard for the weak. They are left to fend for themselves in a world of vultures and self-absorbed individuals. What kind of legacy are we going to leave behind for future generations? What kind of dream inspires most South Africans? These are all things which should concern us as South Africans. The world needs a new value system to come out of Africa. Africa needs to bequeath a new economic system to the world: one that cares for the marginalised of society and yet does not degenerate into state-sponsored socialism.

Death And The NHI

Just over a week ago, I had a conversation with someone which got me thinking about the SA government's proposed National Health Insurance scheme and the potential implications for South African society.

I had a conversation with a man whose wife had just passed away, leaving him the task of raising their children all on his own. It was the circumstances of this woman's death that touched me and got my mind thinking about National Health Insurance in South Africa. One of the organs in this woman's body was badly damaged and had failed, so she was rushed to hospital where the doctors did an incredible job of reviving her and ensuring that she stayed alive.

However, that was only a temporary reprieve because her organ had become so badly damaged that she required a new organ and some surgery if she was going to continue living.

The doctors duly told her husband that a new organ was needed and if the family wanted them to conduct surgery to give this woman a new organ and keep her alive, they would have to pay an exorbitant amount of money. Being from a poor background and having no financial means to raise the required funds the man had to resign himself to the fact that his wife would have to die and there was nothing he could do about it. Without the means to pay for the surgery, the woman passed away and the family was left to mourn and to deal with the effects of her sudden death.

I left the man's company after he told me this whole story wondering what kind of world it is that we live in where the decision whether someone stays alive or not is determined by purely economic factors and not by humanitarian reasons. It struck me as odd that this woman's life could have been saved if she had the right bank balance, but because she didn't, she had to die. I found myself wondering if it is acceptable that we could let someone die just because of a lack of money when the means to save that person are readily available. What happened to all the ideas of human dignity, value, and the sanctity of life? Do we all have a right to live just by virtue of being human or is it also determined by socio-economic factors?

I then began to realise the need for some kind of national health insurance scheme to ensure that unnecessary deaths like this woman's, don't have to occur. Now of course it is common knowledge that the SA government are in the process of launching some kind of national health insurance scheme to ensure universal coverage for each South African citizen and to give poorer citizens access to better quality healthcare. This scheme has typically come under criticism with people questioning its affordability, its viability, and its necessity. A large majority of middle-class South Africans are concerned that they will have to shoulder the burden of financing this health scheme and there have been huge debates about whether we should proceed with national health insurance or not.

From the perspective of the story that I have just related I don't understand how anyone can argue against the need for national health insurance in South Africa. How many people are dying every day whose lives could have been saved if there was some kind of health insurance to cover them but because they can't afford it, they are just simply left to die? Of course, there is genuine concern about the government's ability to run and administer this National Health Insurance scheme as most things that are run by the government in South Africa are in shambles. It seems like everything run by the government is sub-standard and is falling apart, apart from SARS, so one would be rightly justified in questioning the government's ability to implement national health insurance, but this still does not take away the simple fact that some kind of National Health Insurance scheme is needed in South Africa.

This I believe is where the private sector should come in. Given that government is notoriously inefficient and ineffective at delivering services and the need for national health insurance is so blatantly obvious, I believe that we should be looking at finding ways to get the corporate sector to administer and run this National Health Insurance scheme instead of arguing over whether it is necessary or not. It should be obvious that it is unacceptable that people continue to die even when their lives could be saved, just because of affordability issues.

Can The Tide Be Turned?

Sometime during the last week, I found myself having dinner at a hotel restaurant with a few government bureaucrats who are part of the "old school" liberation era ethos and who have served South Africa and her people with integrity, dignity, and commitment over many decades. Invariably after a sumptuous meal, a few glasses of wine and some single-malt whisky, the conversation turned to my favourite topic: politics. We began to talk about the state of politics in South Africa at present, the lived reality of the average South African and how all of this compares to the ideals and principles of our liberation era stalwarts.

The words of the Anglo-Irish poet William Butler Yeats in his famous apocalyptic poem, The Second Coming are most apt in conveying the sentiments that were shared over the dinner table that evening, "things fall apart; the centre cannot hold; mere anarchy is loosed upon the world, the blood-dimmed tide is loosed, and everywhere the ceremony of innocence is drowned; the best lack all conviction, while the worst are full of passionate intensity." The general sentiment expressed was that things were falling apart in the South African body politic, that we had moved away from liberation-era ideals, values, and principles to our detriment as a nation, and that the country had lost its soul and was wandering around purposelessly in need of visionary, inspirational and principled leadership to wake it up from its slumber.

We discussed the rich legacy of principled, values-based leadership that South Africa is blessed with and wondered how we had allowed ourselves to veer away from that. A country that has been blessed with once-in-a-generation leaders like: O.R Tambo, Anton Lembede, Robert Mangaliso Sobukwe, Walter Sisulu, Steve Bantu Biko, Beyers Naude, Bram Fischer, Helen Suzman, Albert Luthuli, Yusuf Dadoo, Ahmed Kathrada, A.P Mda, Moses Kotane, Jan Smuts, Pixley ka Seme etc, all in the last century, should not be struggling with a leadership vacuum like we currently are, surely? The general consensus was that South Africa needs to get back to basics. We need to identify the values, principles, ideals, and aspirations that once made us the envy of the world and we need to put those back at the centre of our society.

It was John Milton who said that "the superior man acquaints himself with many sayings of antiquity and many deeds of the past, to strengthen his character thereby." This is not only true for the individual, but for society as a whole because as the Greek philosopher Plato said, "States are as the men, they grow out of human characters." In other words, if South Africa is going to be the great nation that its rich legacy demands, we are going to need to look back at the past, rediscover the values and ideals that define us as a nation and move forward with that vision in mind. As we were continuing in this vein after supper, my mind began to wander to other concepts and ideas as often happens when I am involved in conversations of this nature.

I remembered the words of that great patriot and exemplary liberation era leader, O.R Tambo, "We seek to create a united, democratic, and non-racial society." It then hit me that the very ideals that Tambo and his generation fought for, are the very ideals that have been under attack and threatened in the "new" South Africa. Our unity as a people has been under attack, as we have allowed ourselves to be pulled apart by all kinds of divisive elements. Our democracy has been under attack as institutions that had been created to safeguard our democracy have been steamrolled by individuals and cabals who have a lust for power and desperation for wealth accumulation at all costs. The ideal of non-racialism has been under attack as a large part of the public discourse has been reduced to nothing but racial arguments. We all need to regather and reclaim this vision of a united, democratic, and non-racial society and to own it and defend it with everything that we have. It is the responsibility of every individual South African to work at building and defending our unity, building and defending our democracy and advancing and promoting non-racialism. That should be the common vision that unites us with our past heroes.

I also remembered the words of the Greek philosopher, Plato, "our object in the construction of the state is the greatest happiness of the whole, and not just that of any one class or group of people." This reminded me of the wonderful miracle of our negotiated transition, the joy of the 1994 elections and that emotional day on 27 April 1994 when Nelson Mandela was inaugurated as the inaugural president of a free and united South Africa. On that great day, we all stood tall as South Africans, recognising that we were entering into an exciting era. The vision that inspired us then was that we were creating a state, a democracy that would be concerned with promoting and upholding "the greatest happiness of the whole." In other words, this new social contract we were entering into promised to look after and promote the interests of all, not some. It wasn't a contract that guaranteed a future for blacks at the expense of whites, rich at the expense of the poor or educated at the expense of the uneducated. It promised something for the whole, not just some parts. This is a vision we need to reclaim as we move forward as a nation and as a people and it should inform all that we are and all that we do because as Ralph Waldo Emerson stated, "what you are comes to you."

I then began to think of the whole modernity project that we began to embark on post-1994 and which became accelerated during the Mbeki presidency. South Africa is a society that is looking to modernise grow, and develop. The things that have characterised modernity in other corners of the globe have been things like liberalism, secularism, pluralism, relativism, materialism, individualism etc. This means that in most societies, the modernity project has meant a move away from conservative values, from absolutes, from focusing on family and society to focusing on individuals, from focusing on individual responsibility to society to focusing on an individual's rights within society etc. It is with the goal of modernising in mind that we created one of the most liberal constitutions in the world.

It dawned on me that maybe what we need to do in some instances is to reverse the effects of modernity and go back to traditional values if we want to fulfil our potential as a nation. For example, we have a large percentage of our population that is dying of AIDS not because the government is not doing its job or condoms don't work, but because we have embraced liberal sexual ethics and values instead of traditional ethics and values when it comes to sex. I mean if people just lived up to the traditional value of waiting, finding one partner, and being faithful to that one partner for the rest of their lives then AIDS wouldn't be such a problem. That is just simple common sense and a return to this simple traditional value would have a massive impact on the future of this nation. Secondly, problems like teenage pregnancies, unemployment, crime etc. could be solved by returning to family values. It has been empirically proven that societies that are founded upon stable family units are more economically productive, and have lower levels of socio-economic problems such as alcoholism, teenage pregnancies etc. So, a return to the promotion of the simple value of family would save us billions of rands in social grants and other expenditures which could be used in more constructive ways. I am aware that this is not all new or original. Still, a glance at South African society and some of its key challenges shows that we have moved away from these traditional values whilst pursuing the goal of modernising that we find ourselves in such troubles. In the words of the poet Robert Frost, "most of the change we think we see in life is due to truths being in and out of favour." We need to reclaim those old truths, those old values as a nation if we are going to overcome our challenges and become the great nation that we aspire to be.

Finally, we need to fight against the phenomenon of commodification and crass materialism that has consumed us all as South Africans. As I was sitting at that dinner table, drinking my wine, I remember this liberation stalwart lamenting at how young South Africans have sold out our liberation era vision by pursuing money and wealth at all costs, with no thought to the kind of people and society that we are becoming. He expressed his sad regret that they had sacrificed their lives for a South Africa which was so inhumane, so driven by money and wealth at the expense of our humanness. The words of the poet William Wordsworth came to mind, "the world is too much with us, getting and spending, we lay waste our powers." I realised that I was part of the problem. I had moved from idealism to crass materialism, and I reflected the very society that was being criticised by the liberation stalwart, that I needed to go back to the basics, to rediscover the values, ideals and principles that made our liberation struggle the most iconic of the twentieth century. The words of the American writer, E.B White came to mind, "I arise in the morning torn between a desire to improve the world and a desire to enjoy the world. This makes it hard to plan the day." I realised that most South Africans are probably stuck in the same dilemma.

I was reminded of the words that had inspired me for most of my life as a young man, uttered by Ernesto "Che" Guevara, "It's all here; an ideal for which to fight coupled with the responsibility of setting an example that doesn't depart from it." And "our only hope is not to give up even one iota of our principles." It is time that we rediscover the values, ideals, and principles that make us great as a nation. It is time that we reclaimed ground from the charlatans who we have allowed to steal in and divert us from the vision of creating a South Africa that can produce a better life for all (not just some).

It is time to go back to the basics. Let us look to the past for inspiration to move towards our common future. Let us do all we can to turn the tide so we can create a South Africa that embraces and celebrates all its peoples as well as giving opportunity to all. In the words of the English poet Alfred Lord Tennyson, "Tis not too late to seek a newer world."

Bring On the Media Tribunal

With the current debate going on in South Africa about the government's plans for a media tribunal, we must revisit the issue of media freedom and its importance for the health of a nation and its democracy.

Media freedom seems to be an issue that has come up quite frequently in recent times on the continent, with a particular focus on countries such as Rwanda, Zimbabwe, and Sudan. It seems that African states are notorious for their contemptuous disregard for media freedom and their dislike for any form of criticism against governing elites. The questions that come to mind are as follows: how important is media freedom for the health of fledgling African democracies? What role should independent, free media play in the development and upkeep of the nation-state? Should the media be held accountable for what they report and how they report it, and if so by whom?

In South Africa, the media seems to have arrogated to itself the role of defenders of our constitutional democracy, by focusing on exposing all forms of government incompetence and corruption. It seems as if media freedom has been reduced to nothing but the freedom to find as many faults as possible with the government and the ruling party, without necessarily contributing anything constructive to the enhancement of the nation-state project. As the English philosopher John Locke said, "It is one thing to show a man that he is in error, and another to put him in possession of the truth." The media seems to be happy to focus on revealing errors without necessarily pointing the way to the truth constructively. The media seems to believe that its freedom is sacrosanct, without necessarily having embraced the responsibility that comes with that freedom.

Surely any form of freedom must have parameters and boundaries within which it operates, otherwise, it becomes destructive. I'm reminded of the Carl Niehaus story which broke last year and the media rightfully exposed Niehaus for the fraud that he is, but at some point, the reporting stopped being about exposing a corrupt public official and became personal, vindictive, and completely destructive. It almost seemed as if the media were out to find out every wrong thing that Niehaus had done throughout his life and to put it in the public forum to completely destroy him without any regard for his humanity. I remember thinking to myself that the media had crossed the line between reporting on a matter of public interest and completely ruining someone. Where was the ethical, responsible reporting in all this?

By the same token when the ANC Youth League came up with allegations of corruption and bribery against some journalists earlier this year, the media completely refused to entertain these allegations on the basis that one of their own was being attacked and that media freedom was under attack as a result. This smacked of double standards as it seemed to indicate that journalists and media people are above reproach simply because of the industry in which they work. I found this to be appalling as we all know that journalists are quick to run with a story and investigate any allegations of corruption against any politician, but when one of their own is attacked suddenly it is an attack on press freedom and we should all be alarmed.

It almost seems as if press freedom is limited to the freedom to attack the government and to find as much fault with the government and ruling party officials as possible. This then calls into question the objectivity of our media and seriously places in doubt the argument for self-regulation that press freedom advocates are always putting forward. As Arthur Schopenhauer said, "Newspapers are the second hand of history. This hand, however, is usually not only of inferior metal to the other hands, it also seldom works properly." To propose that the media should be left to regulate itself is as preposterous as suggesting that the government should be accountable to no one but itself and that it should be a self-regulating mechanism with no external checks and balances. Media, like government is run by people, individuals who are as equally corruptible, equally self-promoting and equally prone to self-preservation as government and public officials are. You don't need to be an expert on human nature to figure this out. The implication is that left to itself, the media, just like the government will run amok and this necessitates an external form of regulation which could easily be the proposed media tribunal in South Africa.

In the words of Friedrich Nietzsche, "Whoever fights monsters should see to it that in the process he does not become a monster." It would appear that the media has become so accustomed to fighting this so-called monster (the government), that the media itself has become an uncontrollable, irresponsible monster, having the power to destroy reputations, careers, lives, and families and yet refusing to be held to account by society. This is the highest form of hypocrisy which the media cannot be allowed to get away with. An independent, free media is an important part of any healthy society, but this independence does not equate to a lack of accountability to society. In the interests of the highly celebrated democratic values of accountability and transparency, the media must allow itself to be regulated externally and there must be an external watchdog that will safeguard the interests of society as relates to the media, just like we demand of politicians and any public servants who have the power to influence society for better or for worse.

The poet W.H. Auden put it so aptly when he said, "What the mass media offers is not popular art, but entertainment which is intended to be consumed like food, forgotten and replaced by a new dish." Media in South Africa has been reduced to nothing but entertainment, with people's lives being dissected and every ounce of their personal lives being splashed across the front pages whilst one may argue that all politicians and public figures should not complain as this is part of the package they sign up for, one has to look at the human cost of some of the irresponsible reporting and to ask oneself whether the kind of society we are trying to build is accurately reflected in this kind of phenomenon. There is a definite distinction between reporting on issues that are of public concern and destroying individual lives under the guise of upholding and defending our democratic freedoms and in many instances, the media tends to cross this line with the self-regulatory mechanism proving ineffective in curbing this kind of cavalier journalism in all its irresponsibility.

To quote the words of Luthando Tofu, "It is much easier for people to believe and embrace what they read or see on television than the very reality in which they live." Given the truthfulness of this statement, the media has a massive impact in terms of affecting people's opinions and outlooks on key issues affecting a nation and for that reason, the media cannot be simply allowed to regulate itself, without some form of external, independent accountability to society, so maybe the call for an official media tribunal is not such a bad thing after all. We can't allow ourselves to place too much confidence in any one of the different pillars that strengthen our democracy (media being one of them) and all these pillars must be independently regulated, to safeguard against the human tendency for self-promotion and preservation and as an important pillar in a healthy democracy, external supervision of the media can only enhance and strengthen its role in society. I end off with the words of the English novelist George Orwell, "early in life I had noticed that no event is ever correctly reported in a newspaper." Bring on that media tribunal!

There Is No Rainbow In South Africa

The recent uproar over comments by government Spokesperson and BMF president Jimmy Manyi about Coloureds and Indians, got me thinking about the concept of a Rainbow Nation and whether the levels of racial integration and interaction in South Africa warrant the label "Rainbow Nation" being given to us as a nation.

I couldn't think about Jimmy Manyi's comments without thinking about Steve Hofmeyer because I think these two have made comments that represent the two extremes that make up contemporary South Africa and punch holes in Mandela's much acclaimed "Rainbow Nation. " In private conversations, I have heard many young black professionals complain about the over-representation of whites in corporate South Africa and how much they get marginalised by these whites who still hold so much power and there is a growing resentment amongst black professionals about the perceived slow pace of change in corporate South Africa despite the many charters that have been drawn up to promote that magical word, "transformation." It is no secret that there is tension between blacks and coloureds in the Western Cape and Indians and Blacks in Durban, so despite the fierce levels of criticism that have been aimed at Manyi for his undoubtedly unwise comments, one can't run away from the fact that his comments represent views that are held by a significant group of blacks, at

126

least in those two parts of South Africa. This is true whether we admit it or not.

I have also heard many white South Africans complain in private conversations about crime, feeling that they are disproportionately targeted which indicates a racial bias and about lack of employment opportunities and perceived racial laws which minimise opportunities for them in contemporary South Africa. A young, black professional who had a private school education and is highly educated, recently told me that he is now looking to change jobs and find a firm where he can work amongst other black people because he and his friends have realised that in the larger firms, they get marginalised by white people. In his words, you, "hit a ceiling and they don't allow you to go higher than that no matter how skilled and competent you are."

An Afrikaner friend of mine recently told me that his people were being deliberately massacred and marginalised in South Africa and that he was "gatvol" and thought they should do something about it. Could it be that Nelson Mandela, despite being critically acclaimed, did us a great disservice by claiming that we were a Rainbow Nation and pushing a false reconciliation which was no reconciliation at all and in so doing allowed us to build on a false foundation which was always going to come crashing down and now the "chickens have come home to roost" and we see how far apart we are despite Mandela's best attempts to pretend otherwise?

We may celebrate Rugby World Cup victories together, we may go to the same schools and universities, we may work in the same companies and shop at the same places but that doesn't a Rainbow Nation make. Maybe the starting point needs to be an honest acknowledgment of the truth that: we are not a Rainbow Nation. We are not united at all. We still live in very separate worlds even when we work in the same places and live in the same suburbs. Our dinner table conversations and fireplace conversations whilst enjoying a braai over the weekend only serve to reveal this deep division.

Our founding fathers and our forefathers always hoped that they would birth a non-racial South Africa, but truth be told we are a long way from achieving that and it is time that we acknowledged that and started dialoguing openly and honestly because this is the only way to build a genuine Rainbow Nation. Despite our best attempts to hide it, the likes of Jimmy Many and Steve Hofmeyer only serve to highlight the fact that there is no Rainbow in South Africa. In writing this I am reminded of a prayer that my great hero Robert Mangaliso Sobukwe prayed whilst being visited by Alex Borraine, lying on his hospital bed, "take away all bitterness from us and help us to work for a country where we will all love each and not hate each other because hate will destroy us all."

Black People Are Murderers

Another week and yet another racial scandal in South Africa. It all started when popular Afrikaner singer Steve Hofmeyer blamed South African blacks for the brutal murder of a farmer: Attie Potgieter, his wife and their three-year-old child. Hofmeyer wrote the following on his Facebook profile, "Blacks (God knows, probably not all of them, but most of those I have observed) feel justified and entitled in everything, from quotas-low matric marks to land-rights brutality. We MUST generalise. Most black people I know are not violent, but they slurp up the propaganda of entitlement. (That's) exactly what gives killers what they need to justify their brutality. I do not know how the world thinks we should transform, integrate and let go of our prejudices and stay nice, tolerant Christians when blacks shoot a three-year-old child in the head. Sorry to emphasise the colour, but I'm struggling to spot the whites who climb over black walls to do that to their children."

These comments by Hofmeyer on his Facebook profile were "liked" by 2070 people (no prizes for guessing the colour of their skin) and he received 791 comments. Elna Strydom's comment was, "You are spot-on. Then the government says farm murders are not racially motivated. Bullshit, of course, they are." Petro Burzler's comment was as follows, "have your say Steve, you are our spokesman. It's time for the racism card to be burnt because it seems it's the only thing that can be spelt." As always there was the usual emotive response on my part to these obviously prejudiced statements.

I wanted to suggest that maybe Hofmeyer needs to expand his circle of black friends because I know many black people who wouldn't sanction the murder of anyone, let alone a three-year-old child, whether directly or indirectly. I wanted to engage in an intellectual debate about how Hofmeyer's statement not only lacked cogency but was invalid as its premise (that black people by their support for the "propaganda of entitlement"), whatever that means, I hope Hofmeyer himself knows the meaning of that phrase, did not support its conclusion that this gives killers the justification they need to brutally murder an innocent family. I wanted to point out that this was at best an untested hypothesis which therefore could not be accepted as fact.

I wanted to point out to Hofmeyer that if he was serious about "being a nice, tolerant Christian even amid blacks shooting innocent, three-year-old white children in the head" then maybe taking Jesus' injunction to "turn the other cheek" might help. Lastly, I also wanted to highlight the fact that Hofmeyer may indeed be struggling to "spot the whites who climb over black walls to do that to their children" but the black majority and I have no struggle whatsoever in seeing a white man who threw a black worker into a lion's den and watched him getting eaten alive, go scot free after spending only five years in prison for his crime, or seeing a hot-headed young Afrikaner youth go into an informal settlement and shoot a few black people dead all because of the colour of their skin or watching a few Afrikaner youths at the University of the Free State urinate into some food, giving that food to a few, old, unskilled black workers to eat, make a video about it and have a few laughs at the expense of these old women. Upon getting caught and exposed, I see the clear silence of the Afrikaner community to this inhumane treatment of poor black workers by these youth and instead, all I see is a race-based defence of their behaviour by the Afrikaner community. Finally, I want to argue to Hofmeyer that the black majority and I have no struggle whatsoever in remembering the inhumane living conditions that most black workers are subjected to by white farmers and the cold reality that most of these white farmers' dogs have better living conditions and are treated with more dignity than poor black workers.

I want to say all these things and more to Hofmeyer and his ilk, but I realise that this will not take us anywhere. This will not help solve the problem and move us forward as a nation. So as offended as I am by Hofmeyer's obviously racially biased, untrue, emotive statement I decided to look beyond it and hear the cry of a people. Perhaps the key is not to address this individual issue on its own but to look beyond the emotion, the untruths, the fabrications, the clear and unjustified bias and generalisation and to hear the genuine concern of a people, the Afrikaner people. A people who are proud, hard-working, who genuinely love South Africa and have a significant role to play in its development. A people who are as authentically African as I and all the other black tribal groups are, who have strengths and weaknesses, unjustified biases and prejudices, fears and concerns just like every other ethnic group. It then dawns on me that perhaps if all of us were able to look beyond the isolated issues and events that invariably bring out our prejudices and our racial biases and we chose to hear the fears and concerns of those who are on the opposite side of the racial divide and to think through how we can address those with immediacy, we would finally find the path to authentic nationhood. Perhaps if we could all do that, we would be able to mourn the murder of a farmer, his wife, and their three-year-old child for what it genuinely is: the tragic and unnecessary death of human beings who have inherent value to us all by their humanity, irrespective of what race they belong to. Perhaps if we all were willing to look beyond how offended we are when racial issues arise and to rather see, feel, and hear the cry of the other racial group, then we could become the South Africa of 1994, the country that stood as the envy of the world, the country that gave the world a practical example of reconciliation, of a people willing to go beyond generations of hatred, mistrust, injustice, and violence to walk together and build a united, prosperous, world-leading nation.

Are We Truly Free?

On Wednesday 27 April, we celebrated Freedom Day in South Africa: 17 years as a genuine democracy with a constitution that guarantees the rights and freedoms of all its peoples.

I spent most of that day indoors, with my economics textbooks, preparing for my upcoming exams and in between I would listen to the radio to keep abreast of current affairs. On one of the popular talk shows on the radio, the issue being discussed was: whether we are truly free as South Africans, 17 years after that momentous day when Nelson Mandela took the oath of office at the Union Buildings, with the whole world watching and with the country excited at this new journey that we were embarking on.

Of course, different people called in and expressed their views on the radio show, with the discussion typically being quite lively and heated. It got me thinking again about freedom and whether South Africa can truly say that it is a nation of "free" people. We live in barricaded, gated houses with boom gates providing entry into most suburbs and yet we claim to be free.

A large percentage of South Africans still have no access to a constant supply of clean water and electricity and yet we brag about our constitution and the rights that it affords its citizens. A majority of South Africans live off government grants and are dependent on the state to provide decent shelter, put food on the table, and get some sort of education and yet we claim to be free. People feel incapacitated to do anything for themselves and sit around waiting for government to do something for them and still, we insist that we are free. I wonder what Steve Biko would think of this kind of "freedom".

We have failed to emancipate our people mentally by giving them a decent education and enabling them to take charge of their own lives and yet we still call ourselves a "free" people. We have not freed ourselves from the racial prejudice that was the foundation upon which the old South Africa was built and yet we dare to celebrate our "freedom." Is freedom simply the right to vote?

Our people now have freedom of movement and can live anywhere they want, as guaranteed by the constitution, but this is all a farce as most South Africans can't afford to buy and own their own houses, so most areas are out of bounds for them. Every year on the 27th of April we celebrate Freedom Day, but how much of this freedom is truly meaningful for the average South African? What does freedom truly look like? Do we even fully understand the concept? Is this what we fought for all these years?

Maybe we need to reassess our position. If the people are not truly empowered to be the captains of their own ships, as is the case in South Africa today, then it makes no sense to celebrate Freedom Day because we only deceive ourselves. The struggle for freedom in South Africa continues and it requires all hands on deck.

An Enemy Called Average

Last week Thursday I had the privilege of attending the Public Sector Excellence Awards at the Sandton Sun in Johannesburg, South Africa. I was invited to these awards as the Editor of Feintandmargin.com and I got the opportunity to rub shoulders with some of South Africa's top technocrats and bureaucrats at the awards ceremony. The purpose of the awards is to honour and acknowledge those public enterprises, organisations, and government departments in South Africa that have done an excellent job of providing quality services and improving the lot of the South African populace. It was encouraging to see that contrary to popular opinion, some great people are working in the South African civil service who are committed to their work, and the country and who do their job with an excellence that is seldom seen in many sectors of South African society. After attending these awards, I began to think about the concept of excellence and its importance for the continent of Africa if the continent's developmental goals are going to be achieved.

The Public Sector Excellence Awards are the brainchild of Thebe Ikalafeng, a man who embodies the spirit of excellence which we need to foster if Africa is going to be turned around during this century. He is also the brains behind another incredible initiative, the Brand Africa Forum which I had the privilege of attending this year and the founder of the industry-leading Brand Leadership Academy in South Africa. Everything this man does reeks of excellence and in my view, he is a prime example of the kind of excellence that Africa needs to nurture but unfortunately so often desperately lacks. As impressive as the awards ceremony was and as inspiring as the whole evening was for me, I did however leave with one or two disappointments which highlighted for me the challenge we face as a continent to embrace the spirit of excellence. Firstly, the awards ceremony started horribly late, because the keynote speaker, Minister in the Office of the Presidency for Performance Monitoring, Evaluation, and Administration, Collins Chabane was fashionably late. This on its own was bad enough but what irked me the most was that no one seemed to take issue with this at all. It seemed to be expected and was treated by many at the function as normal. This struck me as odd. Here we were celebrating excellence and the evening itself was lacking in excellence at a most fundamental level, the keeping of time. It reminded me again of a fundamental problem that we face as Africans in our quest for development and growth. We too easily accept mediocrity without protesting and hence our results tend to be mediocre. As Dexter R. Yaeger Senior put it, "average is nothing more than being the top of the bottom." In the eyes of average people, the average is always considered outstanding and unfortunately, this has come to characterise most of Africa, despite the best efforts of a few amongst us.

Across the continent, in different sectors of society, we see daily examples of this tolerance for mediocrity and substandard work, service and effort which keep the continent from maximising its potential and achieving its developmental objectives. African citizens and African leaders seem to have little or no regard for excellence and as such, much of the continent is stuck in mediocrity and substandard living conditions. The time has come for Africans to demand more of themselves and their leaders by embracing the spirit of excellence and putting off this laissez-faire mediocrity which is common in every sector of African society. To do this there are a few things that we should embrace which would help foster, nurture, and entrench the attitude of excellence necessary to produce the growth needed to put the continent at the centre of human progress. Firstly, there needs to be a renewed focus on working together, a social contract between the public sector, the private sector and individual citizens to put in maximum effort and contribute to meeting the continent's developmental objectives. It cannot simply be left to the public sector, the private sector, and even civil society organisations to do most of the work to turn things around on the continent. Individual citizens need to acknowledge and embrace their responsibility in this regard. Development is highly dependent on an active citizenry which takes proactive measures to bring about change instead of waiting for the government and the private sector to do all the hard work. Along with this social contract, Africa needs to prioritise the setting of goals with non-negotiable timeframes, with rewards for performance and sanctions for non-performance, at every level of African society. This is essential to create and entrench a culture of excellence.

Secondly, there needs to be a focus on problem-solving. Too often in African communities, most of the time is taken up discussing problems and professing doom instead of trying to come up with actionable solutions for the continent's multi-faceted problems. As stated in one article in the Harvard Business Review, "Stop trying to delight your customers, solve their problems." According to Professor Jonathan Jansen, the Vice-Chancellor of the University of the Free State, "That's how you measure excellence, by solving people's problems." Thirdly, there needs to be a renewed focus on efficiency and effectiveness at all levels of African society. We should be putting the most efficient, effective people in the right positions to meet our growth targets. Each African citizen needs to work at becoming more efficient and more effective in all that they do. This is essential because social development and economic growth depend on efficiency and effectiveness.

Fourthly Africa's learning centres and academic institutions need to become centres of excellence, which foster and nurture an attitude and a culture of excellence. A good example of this is the Ghana-India Kofi Annan Centre of Excellence in ICT, which was established in partnership with the Indian government as Ghana's first Advanced Information Technology Institute with the hope of establishing it as a home for the knowledge entrepreneurs of West Africa. It also aims to stimulate the growth of the ICT sector in the Economic Community of West African States (ECOWAS), a regional economic bloc and to provide an enabling environment for innovation, teaching, and learning as well as practical research. The continent needs many more such initiatives and institutions to promote excellence. Another great example of the quest for excellence on the continent is the "Good People, Great Nation" branding initiative in Nigeria, introduced by Professor Dora Nkem Akunyili, Nigeria's Minister of Information and Communications.

Fifthly there needs to be an increased adaptability to change on the continent. Too often Africans are too slow to respond to change and hence get left behind. There also needs to be a focus on "citizen satisfaction" as the primary goal of public service as well as promoting competition to encourage excellence at every level of African society. Finally, we need to focus on building "entrepreneurial governments" on the continent to foster excellence. Entrepreneurial government is defined by Professor Shahida Cassim, the Director of the Centre for Entrepreneurial Studies at the University of Kwazulu Natal, as, "government that is driven by goals rather than rules in the provision of public services, government in which innovation delivers proactive initiatives through delegation of authority and one in which cross-disciplinary and integrated initiatives are commonly found." The following aspects characterise an "entrepreneurial government" according to Professor Cassim:

➢ Citizen participation in the design and delivery of public goods and services

➢ Perceptiveness to change

➢ Fee-for-services entities within the public sector

➢ Use of risk in delivering services

➢ Organisational learning

➢ Knowledge management

➢ Introducing and encouraging innovation

These are some of the aspects we can incorporate into African communities at all levels to bring about the culture of excellence which is sorely lacking. In the words of John Mason, "mediocrity is a region bounded on the north by compromise, on the south by indecision, on the east by past thinking and on the west by a lack of vision." It is time for Africa to rid itself of this enemy called average and to embrace excellence as a way of life.

Responsibilities And Rights

Just under two weeks ago something significant happened in South Africa, which hasn't received the full attention it deserves and which all South Africans who care about building a winning nation should be celebrating much more than we have so far.

The event I am talking about is the launch of the Bill of Responsibilities by Lead SA at Ingqayizivele High School in Tembisa. According to Tony Howard, the CEO of the Independent Group of newspapers in South Africa, this initiative was a "step towards making sure that while we have rights, it is our responsibility as a country to ensure that our rights are upheld." This is a significant step in the continued development of South Africa as a nation because it seeks to entrench a culture of responsibility alongside the culture of rights and dignity that has been promoted post-1994.

One of the great problems facing the post-1994 South African state has been that we have created a society of people who are aware of their rights as individuals but who haven't embraced their responsibility towards themselves, each other and the nation as a whole, and this is something that needs to be curbed if we are ever going to see the progress that we all hope to see as South Africans.

Without a sense of responsibility, a rights-conscious society can easily fall prey to a sense of entitlement which leads to destruction, vandalism, and social disorder. This is what we often see during service delivery protests and trade union marches against wage/salary imbalances. We see people exercising their right to protest irresponsibly and hence these protests often tend towards violence and destructive behaviour. We see people burning schools, looting, attacking the police, and engaging in all sorts of uncivilised behaviour because they have not learnt to exercise their rights responsibly.

We see people demanding free education, free housing, free health care, and jobs without necessarily being willing to do anything for themselves because they have taken on a rights mentality without embracing their responsibilities as citizens. We see ordinary South Africans complaining about the lack of well-paying jobs without being willing to apply themselves to get the education and acquire the skills which are necessary to ensure that they can access those elusive well-paying jobs.

We see people calling for the rolling out of free anti-retroviral and HIV/AIDS medication without being willing to acknowledge that HIV/AIDS is spreading because of irresponsible individual behaviour as opposed to faulty government policies or ineffective awareness campaigns. All these examples are just an indicator of the lack of a culture of responsibility amongst SA citizens. This is why the initiative by Lead SA needs to be celebrated.

We need a Bill of Responsibilities as much as we need a Bill of Rights in South Africa. We need a constitution that emphasises responsibilities as much as it emphasises rights. We need a citizenry that embraces its responsibilities as much as it embraces its rights. As John F. Kennedy famously said in a speech many years ago, "Ask not what your country can do for you, but what you can do for your country." This is the kind of attitude which needs to characterise ordinary South Africans if we are to build a winning nation.

We Are All Corrupt

Sometime during the past week, I was typically reading the South African daily newspapers online when I came across a story that caught my attention and led me to reflect on the issue of corruption and its effect on South African society. The article concerned was about a survey that was done which indicated that a large percentage of South African motorists admitted to having bribed a policeman or a traffic officer at some stage in the last three months to avoid getting a hefty fine or even sterner punishment. This got me thinking about the extent to which corruption runs through South African society and the culpability of ordinary South Africans for this unwanted phenomenon.

If you were to listen to most dinner table conversations or just read South African newspapers you would get the impression that corruption in South Africa is simply a government problem, an ANC problem or at worst an issue that is predominantly found amongst politicians and the political elite, with the rest of South African society being squeaky clean and completely unaffected by it. This is of course quite far from the truth. The inconvenient truth is that you will be hard-pressed to find any South African who has not cut corners at some stage when presented with the opportunity to do so. Most South Africans have bribed policemen and traffic officers at some stage, many in business have been involved in bribery and all sorts of covert activities that have helped them get business or access new markets and opportunities, and many have bought driver's licenses and done all sorts of illegal, underhanded things to get jobs or access opportunities. Corruption is an issue that pervades every level of South African society, despite popular opinion only attributing it to the ANC and the government at large. Frantz Fanon's words most accurately depict the levels of corruption that are prevalent in South Africa today, "the life of the nation is shot through with a certain falseness and hypocrisy, which are all the more tragic because they are so often subconscious rather than deliberate… The soul of the people is putrescent and until that becomes regenerate and clean, no good work can be done." The simple fact is that corruption prevails in South Africa because most of us as citizens are corrupt and easily corruptible and if we were to be honest with ourselves, we would acknowledge that there have been times when we have cut corners and given in to our corrupt nature instead of doing what is right and ethical before the law. As Albert Camus so succinctly put it, "We are all special cases."

The problem is that there is a lot of hypocrisy in our society. We vilify politicians for being corrupt whilst we justify our corrupt behaviour by minimising and downplaying it. In the case of the media, we criticise politicians and the government for not being accountable and open to scrutiny, but the moment that accountability is demanded of us, and the magnifying glass of the nation's eyes is fixed on us demanding greater transparency and accountability to society, we cry foul and claim that our freedoms are under threat. So, we create one standard for politicians and political leaders and expect a different standard to be applied to us out of an exaggerated sense of self-righteousness. This phenomenon reminds me of the words the American poet Walt Whitman uttered about himself, "Do I contradict myself? Very well then, I contradict myself, I am large, I contain multitudes." South Africa has a society and a media that contradicts itself when it comes to the issue of corruption.

The fact that we are such a highly regulated society is just further evidence that we are part of the problem when it comes to corruption. The Greek Philosopher Plato said that "good people do not need laws to tell them to act responsibly, while bad people will find a way around the laws." South Africans have a knack for finding a way around laws even when highly regulated, witness the collusion to fix the bread price that was exposed by the Competition Commission. This is corporate corruption of the vilest kind which directly affected the poorest in society and exploited them for the sake of profit. In the words of the poet William Wordsworth, "The world is too much with us, getting and spending, we lay waste our powers: little we see in nature that is ours." The culture of materialism and wealth accumulation at all costs has infected every sector of South African society and has left a heartless, soulless society in which the popular ethos seems to be, "he who can accumulate the most by whatever means necessary, without ethical or moral considerations, is king."

The lie that we have led ourselves to believe and which the media has popularised is that it is politicians who are evil and corrupt and that they are the only ones who need to be regulated, held to account and scrutinised. This is convenient for all of us, including the media because it keeps us from pointing the finger at ourselves and seeing ourselves as part of the corruption problem in South Africa. The stark reality to paraphrase the words of the philosopher Plato is that "South Africa is what it is because its citizens are what they are." Everyone is pursuing their own personal gain with no regard for ethics and morality, despite our self-deception which has led us to believe that we are not as corrupt as our political leadership. To borrow Ayi Kwei Armah's words from his epic novel, The Beautiful Ones Are Not Yet Born, "Everybody is swimming towards what he wants. Who wants to remain on the beach asking the wind, How... How... How?"

Next time you are sitting around a dinner table and the conversation drifts towards the corrupt escapades of some politician or prominent figure, ask yourself a simple question: how clean am I? Am I totally innocent of corruption or corrupt behaviour? Have I ever bribed or cut corners in my quest for personal advancement and if I have, how different is that from the political figure or public personality that you are vilifying? It is imperative that we continuously remind ourselves of the words of Arthur Schopenhauer in our battle against corruption and its destructive effects, "national character is only another name for the particular form which the littleness, perversity, and baseness of mankind take in every country."

Constitutional Court Judgement Reveals Value Misalignment

The Constitutional Court judgement upholding a high court ruling that corporal punishment at home is unconstitutional, meaning that it is illegal for parents to use the common law defence of moderate and reasonable chastisement to discipline their children through spanking, has got South Africans talking and apart from silly, but funny social media jokes about things like, whether the judgement applies to spanking during consensual sex between two adults as couples often refer to each other as "baby", there are a lot of serious issues that have arisen as a result of it.

Apart from the merits and demerits of the judgement, which I am not qualified nor inclined to comment on, what struck me the most was the fact that Chief Justice Mogoeng Mogoeng has once again proven himself to be a profound constitutionalist, able to pass a judgement which goes against his Christian convictions but is in line with the values and ideals of our much-celebrated constitution in a pluralistic, modern secular humanist state advancing liberal as opposed to traditional, conservative values.

One wonders what happened to all the naysayers who criticised Mogoeng's appointment unfairly on the basis that he holds conservative, Christian values as if to suggest that as a professional who just so happens to be Christian, he was incapable of separating his own value system and inclinations from those of the Constitution of the Republic if needs be. The judgement is in line with the sentiments expressed by American novelist Richelle E. Goodrich in her book Smile Anyway, "Our greatest duty to our children is to love them first. Secondly, it is to teach them. Not to frighten, force, or intimidate our children into submission, but to effectively teach them so that they have the knowledge and tools to govern themselves."

What intrigued me the most about the judgement was also what it said about modern South African society and its acclaimed constitution. It's interesting to note how highly behavioural theories are influencing the type of society we live in. It's also quite eye-opening to realise how lacking in self-governance we are as a people, hence basic things such as principles of raising a child have to be regulated by a nanny state. It is because of this lack of self-regulation for example that government has to spend so much money and resources dealing with behavioural issues such as practising safe sex. So, we see the state increasingly involving itself in private matters such as people's sexual behaviour, because there is little or no self-governance in South African society. Hence the high crime rate amongst many of our other social ills. As blogger and author T.F Hodge puts it, "rules, laws, and codes become obsolete amongst the self-governed."

Now, I am no advocate for Bakunian anarchy, but all this interests me in terms of how we as citizens relate to the state in this constitutional dispensation that we find ourselves in. Another aspect that I started thinking about when observing the discourse on this judgement, was how much of a disjuncture there is between some foundational principles of our constitution and a large part of the constituency in South Africa.

So, you find things that are against the values of the constitution oftentimes being at loggerheads with the values of most of the South African constituency. In simple terms, a constitution of liberal values of a secular humanist nature often finds itself at odds with the traditional, conservative values that most of the South African constituency espouses and hence you have such an uproar when such a judgement is given, apart from intellectual, secular humanist elites who are the drivers of the current constitutional model anyway.

A good mate of mine reminded me that a constitution is idealistic, representing where we want to go as a society not necessarily where we are, as an explanation for the current discrepancy. I asked whether there shouldn't be an amalgamation of values and principles of what we want to be as a people, before setting this ideal. Now, holding traditional, conservative values doesn't make one anti-constitutionalism, don't get me wrong, but rather it is these liberal, secular humanist values that are underpinning our constitution that often create problems.

So as conservative and religious lobby groups are up in arms over this judgement, it behoves us to remind ourselves that what they represent, is the value system and interests of most of the South African population who have not yet adopted the values of this elite, secular humanist constitutional project of liberal values that we have embarked on. Of course, democracy is not akin to majoritarianism, as majorities can often be wrong as history has proven, but this is an interesting angle that we must interrogate even as we consider the merits and demerits of the Constitutional Court judgement.

The State of the Nation

With the current battle going on between the government and the fourth estate over media rights and the perceived threat to our young democracy of the proposed media tribunal, we must reflect on the current state of the nation of South Africa and the health of our developing democracy.

The key benchmarks to look out for in this regard would be what Brian Pottinger, the author of the book, The Mbeki Legacy, has termed the four important checks in a state, namely: 1) an informed and vigilant polity 2) competent press 3) a strong and incorruptible democracy and 4) an independent parliament and a fearless judiciary with integrity.

With regards to the first check: an informed and vigilant polity, it is quite evident that South Africa as it stands, falls short of the levels of engagement required of its citizens, if it is indeed going to be a healthy democracy. It was the American poet Walt Whitman who said that "a great city (nation) is that which has the greatest men and women." The South African populace is neither informed nor vigilant enough to safeguard and strengthen its budding democracy. South Africa's electorate is highly unsophisticated and lacks the education and intellectual capacity required to hold its political leadership accountable to the extent that is required to ensure a healthy democracy.

The failure of the education system to educate its citizens to the levels required to produce an informed and vigilant polity and the clear lack of interest of the population in acquiring a decent education is a clear threat to the development of democracy in this country. It reminds me of the comment made by Lord Salisbury when someone suggested that the poor be given free libraries, "they don't want libraries, give them a circus." Whilst many are quick to blame the ANC government for the failure of the education system in this country a proper analysis of the situation will reveal that there is a huge disregard for the value of education amongst the citizenry and a severe lack of interest in taking the necessary steps to become a more informed, vigilant polity. In the words of the American poet Ezra Pound, "real education must ultimately be limited to men who insist on knowing, the rest is mere sheepherding." What we currently have in South Africa is a populace that is not interested in knowing and as a result has just become mindless sheep being herded by opportunistic politicians. The people are happy to be part of a political circus and to be led by fanatics who don't have their best interests at heart. As the philosopher Friedrich Nietzsche put it, "Fanatics are picturesque; mankind would rather see gestures than listen to reasons." South Africa falls short of the requirement of having an informed and vigilant polity to ensure the health of its democracy.

The second important check in a state is the nurturing, promoting, and developing of a competent, accountable press to safeguard its democracy. Contrary to popular opinion, as advocated by the press, the biggest threat to media freedom in South Africa is not the ANC-led government, but the press itself. Despite its many successes in exposing corruption and incompetence in government, the South African press is largely characterised by blandness, incompetence and an alarming distance from the majority who make up the population of the country. The media reports in such a manner that it does not necessarily inform the majority of the populace but instead represents the sectional interests of a small middle class which is not necessarily patriotic but is primarily concerned with protecting its class interests and creating opportunity and defending the space it has created for itself for wealth accumulation at the cost of the health of society as a whole. Whenever the spotlight is placed on the media and its incompetence is brought to the fore, the media simply gets defensive and cries wolf, claiming that democracy is under attack instead of working at improving itself and serving society better in a manner that will spread democracy to all corners of South Africa and not just to the select few who make up the educated economic elite.

Whilst doing a decent job of keeping government accountable and keeping public servants honest, the jury is still out on whether the press in South Africa is competent, effective, and objective enough to contribute towards the health of its democracy constructively instead of being just antagonistic towards the government. This would require the press to take up its mandate to ensure that it caters for a larger percentage of the population than it currently does and to work at spreading knowledge and information to all corners of South Africa in creative ways instead of just catering for sectional, minority interests as it currently does.

The third aspect that we need to look at in gauging the health of our democracy is the issue of building a strong and incorruptible democracy by creating state institutions that guard against the natural human propensity to be corruptible, in a non-partisan manner. The biggest problem in South African society at present is the seemingly popularly held view that corruption in South Africa is a phenomenon that can only be found in the ANC-led government and its alliance partners and that if we got rid of the ANC and its allies corruption would disappear in South Africa. This is a clear fallacy as corruption is common to the human race as a whole and can be found in all sectors of South African society even amongst the media and the opposition parties that self-righteously claim to be above-board and focus on exposing corruption in the ANC and government without tackling it as a society-wide problem that threatens to destroy our democracy as materialism and a get-rich-at-all-costs mentality seems to have taken over South Africans at every level of society, hence the high levels of crime of all sorts.

The solution is to create a political system which ensures that whoever governs and leads South Africa is directly accountable to the people and is forced to govern transparently and openly. The proportional representation parliamentary system which South Africa has adopted is not the best at ensuring this direct accountability. This system has meant that no politician is directly accountable neither to a particular constituency nor to the electorate, but rather to the party. This has given party apparatchiks disproportionate power and influence which has been abused by all political parties and political leaders in South Africa to dispense patronage and to ensure loyalty and votes in party elections.

The governing party itself has been guilty of dismantling whatever institutions had been set in place to safeguard our democracy, in the pursuit of wealth and personal enrichment for the political elite. State institutions that should have been protected and promoted to create a democratic culture and a democratic legacy for future generations have been compromised just so that a small minority can benefit materially. The government has done everything it can to prove the truthfulness of Adam Smith's words that, "there is no art which one government sooner learns of another than that of draining money from the pockets of the people."

This demonstrates a clear failure by the ANC-led government to recognise its responsibility to ensure that it creates and promotes a democratic culture by respecting state institutions and placing them above party structures, to leave a democratic legacy for future generations just like we saw with the founding fathers in America at the formation of the American union. As Charles de Montesquieu put it, "In the infancy of societies, the chiefs of state shape its institutions; later the institutions shape the chiefs of state." By its overwhelming majority and given the fact that we are still a young, developing democracy this is a responsibility that the ANC needs to take up with vigour to safeguard our democracy and ensure its future. Sadly, this is an area in which the party has failed spectacularly to the detriment of our democracy.

Finally, the fourth aspect that we need to consider in analysing the state of our democracy is ensuring that we have an independent parliament and a fearless, independent judiciary with integrity. We have already discussed the problem of parliamentarians being accountable to the party and not to the people and how this affects their independence. The issue of the judiciary in South Africa is a very complex one because whilst there has been evidence of judicial independence and a willingness to make decisions that go against the executive to uphold the constitution, there has also been evidence of judges being involved in helping certain political factions in their battles against their opponents in petty succession squabbles within the ruling party and this has to some extent undermined the confidence the citizenry has in the judiciary and its impartiality. Like almost every sector of South African society, the judiciary seems to have become highly politicised and lacking in impartiality, which is a great threat to our budding democracy.

An objective analysis of the current state of our nation and the health of its democracy reveals many worrying signs of ill health and places a huge responsibility on each South African to play an active role in building and enhancing democracy for the sake of future generations. As the novelist Robert Tressell so aptly put it in his novel The Ragged Trousered Philanthropists, "Every man who is not helping to bring about a better state of affairs for the future is helping to perpetuate the present misery and is, therefore, the enemy of his own children. " We have a duty to ensure that we take whatever steps are necessary individually and corporately so we can become a nation with an informed, vigilant polity; a competent, accountable press; a strong and incorruptible democracy based on an unshakeable confidence in democratic institutions and not on individuals and political parties and finally an independent parliament (which might require that we push for electoral reform) as well as an independent judiciary that is fearless, objective, and depoliticised.

A Necessary Change In Political Culture

The sentencing this week of a good mate of mine, Fees Must Fall activist, Mcebo Freedom Dlamini, got me thinking about the protest culture in this country and the need for a change in our general political culture. The right to protest is enshrined in our constitution, but often we find that communities burn public infrastructure and commit violent acts when protesting to defend their rights, forgetting that rights do indeed come with responsibilities, which we must always honour in whatever protest action we partake in.

There is a serious need for a change in political and protest culture in this country, because unlike in the 1980s, we are no longer fighting to bring down an unjust regime, but rather, within the post-94 dispensation, we are trying to build a country, in an inclusive and socially cohesive manner.

The challenge we are faced with, of deconstructing remnants of the colonial and apartheid legacy in our society, is also counteracted by the fact that, simultaneously, we are also building a new society, that is socially inclusive and cohesive for the benefit of all South Africans. My friend Mcebo's sentencing this week, for his actions during the Fees Must Fall protest movement, a just struggle if ever there was one, brought this home in the most personal manner.

It highlighted the need for a change in political culture, and a new ethos within our communities, taking us from a "struggle" mindset to a nation-building outlook. This will affect how we protest and register our dissatisfaction with any aspects of our democratic establishment. It will bring about respect for the rule of law and our constitutional mechanisms, which should ensure that the days of burning down buildings and public infrastructure as we did in the 1980s when we exercised our right to protest, are at an end.

No matter how just our cause is, respect for order and the rule of law is a non-negotiable for any sane society. Public backlash against ineptitude and corruption, which lead to service delivery lags, should never degenerate into the lawlessness we often witness when our communities protest. This lawlessness is also seen in the problem of illegal land invasions and occupation of houses that the government has built for families within our communities.

Dissatisfaction with corrupt activity and inefficiencies, which delay the delivery of houses to worthwhile beneficiaries should never degenerate into the lawlessness that we are seeing with these illegal land invasions and occupation of houses and the criminal cartels that are behind them.

Part of the change in political culture will also require embracing a new service delivery model, with communities rightly expecting that the public representatives that they have elected into office through their political parties, will deliver basic services and public goods of the highest quality. That is a reasonable expectation, which unfortunately goes unmet all too often in contemporary South Africa.

With this expectation, must also come a new attitude from our communities, not seeing themselves as passive recipients within the service delivery process, but rather as partners and ultimately the most critical stakeholders in that process, who are also active participants in that process. This perspective, of course, will create opportunities to promote local SMMEs and entrepreneurs and local economic development, throughout the value chain of the service delivery process.

This should enable the delivery of cost-effective, efficient, effective services to local communities, of course with the implication that corruption and middlemen entities, with their parasitic, rent-seeking tendencies are dealt with and removed from the equation, something that we have not been very good at, or honest about addressing to be more accurate.

Building something is always more hard work than breaking it down, so as we exercise our right to protest and defend our rights as citizens and communities, it behoves us to constantly remind ourselves that we are in a different dispensation, requiring a different ethos and outlook and hence we should not be destroying public property or committing acts of criminality and violence in doing so.

4

Africa: The Final Frontier

Oscar Wilde And the New African Movement

Over the past week, I have been reading Oscar Wilde's six hundred-page biography and have been enthralled and inspired by the life and times of one of the most iconoclastic individuals to have ever walked on planet Earth. Apart from being an incredibly interesting individual, Wilde was also the leader of a movement that was dubbed the "Aesthetic movement" which purported to have found the answer to man's eternal quest for meaning and aimed to provide a new sense of purpose, definition, and identity for man.

Wilde's "aesthetic philosophy" can best be defined in his own words, "to treat life in the spirit of art is to treat it as a thing in which means and end are justified, to witness the spectacle of life with appropriate emotions." This idea of redefining the meaning of life and the purpose of human existence under the title of "Aestheticism" got me thinking about the need for a "New African Movement."

The "New African Movement" would be about redefining Africanness and putting Africa at the forefront of civilisation and the quest for human progress. The "New African Movement" would be made up of Africans who are the most inventive, innovative, and creative people. The "New African" would be self-driven, independent, and free from bondage to tradition and be committed to making his contribution to the quest for mankind's progress.

The "New African" would be self-regulating, visionary, and focused on legacy instead of subsistence. He would be multi-generational in thinking, perspective, and outlook and would be entrepreneurial on a macro rather than just a micro level. This "New African" movement would seek to define the 21st-century African and in so doing put Africa at the centre of world progress. It's time that we redefined the concept of Africanness and freed it from its colonial baggage, its racist inclinations and its pitiful connotations.

It's only the "New African" who can produce a "New Africa" and the time for the "New African" to emerge is now. The call for a "New African" movement is more than a call for self-determination but is rather a desire for a fresh start for the continent emanating from within the African himself. It also goes beyond the calls for a Renaissance or an awakening as this is often nothing more than a rehashing of old themes and a resurrection of tired arguments and philosophies that have made the continent backward and peripheral.

The "New African" movement would be built on evolutionary concepts rather than static mystical beliefs and would focus more on citizenship than leadership to create an Africa of responsible and responsive individuals. The only way the fate of the continent will change in the 21st century is if this "New African "were to emerge and begin to actively work at creating a New Africa.

The New Africa

Watching events unfold in Libya, Zimbabwe, Ivory Coast, and a few other places on the continent reminded me of the words of Algy Cluff, the founder of Cluff Resources, "being in love with Africa is like being in love with a woman who does not love you back. You feel like bursting into tears at times." Like the old cliché says, the more things change the more they stay the same.

What we are witnessing in Libya, Zimbabwe, and the Ivory Coast is a scene that has frustratingly played itself out on too many occasions on the continent. We have a typical African strong man refusing to let go of power even when it is clear that the will of the people is that he should step down and it looks like the outside world is powerless to do anything about this or perhaps just lacks the political will to change things. The very same words that Robert Sobukwe used to describe post-colonial Africa at a time when African countries were starting on a journey of independence can still be used today to describe the Africa we live in today, only this time these words describe, not the actions of outsiders against Africans, but Africans against Africans, "we are witnesses today of cold and calculated brutality, the desperate attempts of a dying generation to stay in power. We also see a new spirit of determination, quiet confidence, the determination of a people to be free whatever the cost."

We are seeing an old generation of post-colonial African leaders refusing to let go of the levers of power even when it has become clear that there is a new wave that is spreading across the continent, a new force for freedom, a new confidence that has come upon the African citizen that change is indeed possible, that Africa need not be characterised by despotism, autocracy, violence, and death any longer. The post-colonial African generation of leaders continues to hold the continent back and seeks to stifle the momentum that has been built around this push for a new Africa. The civilian protests that have brought about change in North Africa are an indication of this new zest for freedom that has come upon Africans. Even as we see resistance to this push for change in places such as Zimbabwe, Swaziland, Ivory Coast etc. we must rally around this movement towards a new Africa.

We need to be able to see beyond the temporary obstacles presented by a generation that has stayed in power for too long and actively work at promoting this new Africa. We need to be like the ex-Robben Island prisoner DM Zwelonke and his peers who saw a new Africa amid oppression and suppression. To use Zwelonke's own words, "Our minds would be filled with vision, and we would see a new Africa we so much yearned, so much suffered for, being just around the corner... we needed to see the silver lining in the dark clouds of suppression that so dangerously hung over our heads."

The winds of change are blowing through the continent once again and the call for a young generation of Africans to arise and take the continent on a different trajectory has gone forth. As Robert Sobukwe famously said, "It is necessary for human progress that Africa be fully developed and only the Africans can do so. We want to build a new Africa and only we can build it." It is time for Africans of all sorts to arise and contribute towards building this new Africa. An Africa that is fully independent and self-determined. An Africa which is founded on the full development of the African, an Africa which is defined more by what it stands for than what it stands against. Post-colonial Africa has too often been defined by what it stands against rather than what it stands for: anti-colonialism, anti-imperialism, anti-Apartheid etc. This is insufficient to build the Africa we want in the 21st century. As Bob Sobukwe said, "I wish to make it clear again that we are anti-nobody. We are pro-Africa. We breathe, we dream, we live Africa; because Africa and humanity are inseparable."

Too often the post-colonial discourse and policy framework in Africa has been informed by what the African is against rather than what the African stands for. The time for that has passed. It is time to focus on building a new Africa with a positive vision that is not informed by a tainted past, an Africa that takes its rightful place within the context of the global human family. To quote Bob Sobukwe again, "World civilisation will not be complete until the African has made his full contribution. And even as the dying so-called Roman civilisation received new life from the barbarians, so also will the decaying so-called western civilisation find a new and purer life from Africa."

The global push for democratic change that has been inspired by the courage and sacrifice shown by young North Africans in tackling tyranny is indicative of the kind of contribution that Africa can make towards creating a better world in the 21st century, it is indicative of the capacity of the African to be at the forefront of the quest for human progress and development. As we witness the epoch-defining clashes of the African to extricate himself from tyrannical leadership and the ills of a closed society and the stubborn refusal of the post-colonial African generation to let go of power and usher in a new era of freedom, let us constantly remember the words of Robert Mangaliso Sobukwe, "let me plead with you, lovers of my Africa to carry with you into the world the vision of a new Africa, an Africa reborn, an Africa rejuvenated, an Africa recreated, young Africa. We are the first glimmers of a new dawn. The wheel of progress revolves relentlessly, and all the nations of the world take their turn at the field-glass of human destiny. Africa will not retreat! Africa will not compromise! Africa will not relent! Africa will not equivocate! And she will be heard! Remember Africa!"

More Suarez, Less Gyan Please!

The recent debacle over the conduct of Luis Suarez of Uruguay in the football World Cup quarter-final game between Uruguay and Ghana got me thinking again about the African psyche and the reasons why Africa still lags behind the rest of the world in so many different fields. Unlike many of my African brethren, I was not necessarily saddened by Uruguay's victory in that game even though I had supported Ghana and had wanted them to progress to the semi-finals of the World Cup. I found myself torn between my desire to see an African team progress to the semi-finals of the football World Cup for the first time and my desire, as a football traditionalist to see a traditional football powerhouse such as Uruguay finally awakening, after so many years in the football wilderness. Being a history lover and a traditionalist of some sort in these things, for me it was great to see a nation with such a great history and football pedigree as Uruguay finally taking its rightful place amongst the elite footballing nations of the world again. Secondly, after many years of sincerely believing that Diego Forlan was one of the most underrated players in the world, I was glad that he was finally getting the opportunity to showcase his talent on the biggest stage of all and to also stake his claim to being placed amongst the elite footballers of the world in the modern era.

It was for these reasons that Uruguay's victory over Ghana was a bitter-sweet experience for me. It also contained many lessons for us as Africans of what it takes to win in the world that we live in and what we will need to do if we are going to turn Africa around in the twenty-first century. Luis Suarez was vilified and branded a cheat for handling a goal-bound ball in the last seconds of the game against Ghana and in so doing keeping Uruguay's hopes of making the World Cup semi-finals alive. Africans all over complained, bemoaning how Ghana was cheated out of a deserved semi-final spot and how much of an injustice was done in that game. In doing so many Africans forgot to apportion blame where it was justly deserved, and this revealed to me a typical African weakness which I believe is one of the reasons why Africa still lags behind the rest of the world at the beginning of the twenty-first century. What Suarez did, did not cost Ghana the game. Suarez handled the ball, was sent off and a penalty was awarded. This means that in footballing terms, justice was served. The player who deliberately handled the ball was sent off and Ghana were awarded a penalty which would have allowed them to win the game and proceed to a World Cup semi-final for the very first time. In other words, despite what Suarez had done, it was still within the hands of a Ghanaian player to ensure that Ghana progressed to their first World Cup semi-final. This responsibility was handed over to Ghanaian striker Asamoah Gyan. Of course, we all know that he missed the penalty, Ghana lost the subsequent penalty shootout and Uruguay progressed to the World Cup semi-finals.

What was interesting for me was the reaction of most Africans to this undoubtedly emotional defeat. Many Africans were quick to blame Suarez for Ghana's defeat and to pull out the victim card, saying that Ghana had been cheated out of a World Cup semi-final spot. This was not just highly inaccurate, but a gross distortion of the facts. As insensitive as it may sound, Ghana lost that match, not because they were cheated, but because their striker and key penalty taker, Asamoah Gyan, missed a penalty he should have scored which would have taken his team through to the semi-finals. If anybody was to blame for Ghana's loss, it was him, not Suarez. Suarez did everything that his countrymen would have expected him to do to ensure that his team went as far as they could in the World Cup, but Gyan didn't. In the final analysis, after all the complaining and whingeing, the end result was that Uruguay was through to the World Cup semi-finals and Ghana was out. In typical African fashion, we found it easier to blame an outsider for failure than to place the blame squarely at an African's feet for not doing his job when it was required of him to do so. This is the same mentality that we see across Africa when people are asked to explain what is wrong with the continent.

We find it easier to blame colonialism, the Europeans, the Americans, slavery etc. than to blame ourselves and to take responsibility for where we are as Africans. Whilst not meaning to downplay the effects of all these external factors in Africa's continued impoverishment, the reality is that Africa has failed to develop post-independence not just because of the above factors but mainly because of corrupt African leaders, dictators, and despots who have ravaged their countries and their peoples for personal gain (and in many instances been allowed to do so by African citizens to the point of even excusing and defending their behaviour in some instances), civil wars consisting of one African faction fighting against another African faction (using European manufactured weapons, but nonetheless still African against African), economic mismanagement by African governments (even though there were structural adjustment programmes imposed on African governments by the IMF and the World Bank there was still gross economic mismanagement within African governments), narrow-minded tribalism and ethnicism (although the roots of these are often traced directly to Europe and colonialism, the fact remains that Africans could still have acted differently and in a more humane manner towards each other post-independence, with the broader goal of nation-building in mind) etc. In other words, just like with the Ghana versus Uruguay example, despite the external factors, it was still within the control of African citizens and their leaders to build successful, winning nations post-independence, but most didn't and ended up plundering and looting their countries whilst blaming the West for their plight. This is a trait that we need to lose as Africans if we are indeed going to modernise and develop in this century. You see despite what Suarez did or did not do, Ghana could (and should) have still won that game if their player had done his job, which is to score the penalty. In the same way, Africa could still have developed and modernised post-independence despite the scourge of colonialism, neo-colonialism and all forms of exploitation, if her leaders and her citizens had made different choices and consciously followed a different path. It was still within Africa's control, and it is still within Africa's control to follow a different growth trajectory if we make better choices and stop passing blame.

It was interesting for me that people found it easier to blame Suarez than Gyan after Ghana's loss. The reality is that the world does not work like that if you want to be a winner. The world sympathises with the Gyan's and Ghana's of this world but in the end, the bottom line is what matters and after all the tears and sympathy, the results that are attained through the work of the Suarez's of this world still stand. We have to decide as a continent whether we want to be a continent that the world feels sorry for, or we want to be a continent of winners. If we want to be winners, then we need to produce more Suarez's. If we want to be a continent that the world looks on with pity (as has been happening over the past fifty years) then we will continue to produce more Gyan's and to excuse and celebrate their failure. Suarez represents the kind of person who gets things done, who produces results despite criticism and vilification, who will do whatever it takes to advance the cause of his country, and who is ruthlessly efficient and effective. This is the kind of person required if Africa is going to arise in the twenty-first century. Gyan represents the incompetent, pitiful African who despite being afforded the opportunity can never quite break out of his shell and seems to have a ceiling when it comes to what he can accomplish or achieve, the African who somehow cannot compete on the global scale and is always found wanting at critical moments, the African who can't take responsibility for his failures and short-fallings, but instead looks for excuses and sympathy when he realises that he doesn't quite match up, the African who will garner the world's sympathy, receive aid, always be the also-ran on the global stage etc. This is the kind of leadership and citizenry that has characterized Africa over the past fifty years and is one of the primary reasons why Africa is where it is at the moment.

The world is a ruthless place. There is no room for sentiment and emotionalism on the world stage. It is results that matter and if Africa is going to maximise its potential, we will need to embrace some of that ruthless streak. Now I am not saying that we should abandon all ethics and morality in the quest for growth and development for Africa in the twenty-first century, but I am saying that we need to be more ruthlessly efficient, more one-track-minded, more results-oriented, less tolerant of failure (even glorious failure), less accepting of mediocrity, offer fewer excuses and take more responsibility. In the footballing example I have been using so far, Suarez did what he had to do to keep his country in the tournament, but Gyan didn't. That is the bottom line. Whatever sense of injustice and unfairness we may or may not have felt, it was still within the African's hands to ensure his team went through and when it was required of him to step up, take responsibility and produce results, he did not. It is the same for Africa in so many other spheres. Whatever injustices there have been in the past and whatever injustices are still festering upon us in the current era, often when Africans are required to step up, take responsibility and produce results, we fail and then blame others for our failure. This is not the winning mentality that produces winning nations. If we want to be at the forefront of world civilization and to lead the world in terms of growth and development in the twenty-first century, then the formula is really simple: more Suarez, less Gyan, please!

Mandela Or Zuma: Just More of The Same

It was interesting to me as I was reading one of the South African weeklies last week; to read the story about Nelson Mandela and the two women who it is claimed are his as yet unacknowledged children. According to the information given, the Nelson Mandela Foundation has already verified that one of the women, who has just recently passed away, was indeed Mandela's daughter and the other woman's claim is still being investigated.

This whole story reminded me of the furore over President Jacob Zuma fathering a child out of wedlock, which broke a while back and I found myself comparing our beloved Saint Nelson with our incumbent president and seeing no real difference. I know this will shock a lot of people since there seems to be this unspoken rule that Saint Nelson should be treated as some sort of deity whilst the likes of Zuma and his contemporaries are nothing but trouble and should be treated with utmost disdain and suspicion as they symbolise everything that is wrong with South Africa whilst Saint Nelson epitomises all that we aspire to be as a nation.

The truth of the matter is that both men fathered children, with different women out of wedlock (you could argue that Mandela's case is different since he was younger when he fathered these children, but the effect is still the same). Both stories broke out in the media, and it has been interesting for me to observe the varying responses of the media and society to these stories. Of course, President Zuma, being the evil, irresponsible guy (at least that's how the media often portrays him) was vilified whilst there has been a hush about the Mandela story and the plight of the two women who are supposedly his long-lost children.

The whole saga got me thinking about the concept of "heroes" and the role they play in the make-up of society and the promotion and advancement of the aspirations and ideals of "the people." I got to thinking about this because the Mandela story made me realise that as saintly as many people think Mandela is, he is no different from the average South African male who has sired children out of wedlock and is notorious for his womanising ways. In other words, our leaders and our "heroes" are nothing but a reflection of what we already are as a people; they reflect to us what we truly are.

I then began to ask myself some key questions: why do we place so much trust in "heroic" individuals to deliver us and take us forward? Why are we always looking towards some "great figure" to take us towards our Promised Land? It then dawned on me that part of the problem with Africa is that we have placed too much confidence in these "heroes" and figureheads and this has largely kept us from taking charge of our own lives and our destinies and has left us completely disempowered as a result. Africa is full of great "heroes" who have been acclaimed as the "saviours" of their nations, but is short of great citizens who take charge of their own lives and do not look to someone external to help them live out their dreams and aspirations. If Africa is going to become a fully functional, prosperous continent, this "hero-worship" must be forsaken and instead, we need to focus on building societies made up of empowered citizens who have the capacity within themselves to make their dreams come true.

This reliance or dependence on "great heroes" of course then translates into an over-dependence on political parties and politicians to bring about the necessary changes that will help citizens attain their goals and fulfil their aspirations. Of course, this is not a uniquely African phenomenon. The euphoric election of Barack Obama to the position of American president had clear elements of this "hero-worship" as Obama was treated like some kind of messianic figure who would radically transform Washington, clean up government and ensure a better deal for the average American. This was a hugely unfair and unrealistic expectation that no man could ever have lived up to (and Obama hasn't).

The Chinese had Mao Tse-Tung and Deng Xiaoping, the Cubans had "El Jefe Maximo" Fidel Castro, the Turks had Mustafa Kemal Ataturk and the list goes on and on for different parts of the world. It seems as if there is an innate human desire to create heroes and messiahs who will "take us out of our plight" but as Albert Camus put it, "every revolutionary ends up either by becoming an oppressor or a heretic" or in the words of Ralph Waldo Emerson. "Every hero becomes a bore at last."

Africa is full of tales of great "heroes" who became heretics, oppressors, and complete bores once they had tasted the fruits of power and the benefits of controlling access to resources and opportunities. One of the biggest stumbling blocks to progress in Africa has been this over-reliance on these "heroes" and "father figures" to lead us to that Promised Land of prosperity and progress that we all yearn for and if we are going to see a change in Africa's fortunes in the twenty-first century, this is one of the tendencies that we are going to have to let go off.

According to the author James Davison Hunter in his book, To Change the World, "most of us are inclined to what has been called the Great Men (Great Person) view of history. It is a Hegelian idea of leadership and history, popularised by the nineteenth-century Scottish historian, Thomas Carlyle. In his own words, the history of the world is nothing but the biography of great men, for universal history, the history of what man has accomplished in this world, is at the bottom the history of the Great Men who have worked here. They were the leaders of men, these great Ones; the modellers, patterners and in a wide sense creators, of whatsoever the general mass of men contrived to do or to attain; all things that we see standing accomplished in the world are properly the outer material result, the practical realisation and embodiment, of thoughts that dwelt in the Great men sent into the world." Whilst it could be argued that there are elements of truth in the above statement, the problem with that particular view is that it disempowers society, leaves the quest for progress and development in the hands of a few people, it leaves the majority on the periphery. It breeds populations and citizens who are over-dependent on politicians and the state to meet their immediate needs and desires. It leads to inaction and a lack of initiative and dynamism amongst the populace.

It is my conviction that Africa needs great, ordinary citizens much more than it needs Great Men. The Greek philosopher Plato put it well when he said, "This city (state) is what it is because our citizens are what they are." Africa's failings so far are more a failing of citizenship than a failing of leadership. It is the average, ordinary citizen's over-reliance on some mythical, heroic political figures that has allowed elites to plunder resources and live opulently whilst the common man on the streets is battling to make ends meet. To ensure progress and change in Africa we need to focus on producing great citizens instead of focusing on producing great leaders and great figureheads because ultimately the leadership will only be a reflection of the society from whence it hails. To paraphrase the words of the American poet Walt Whitman, "produce great citizens, the rest will follow."

Mandela or Zuma, Tsvangirai or Mugabe, Kaunda or Chiluba, Mobutu or Kabila, Bush or Obama, Thatcher or Blair: it is all the same. Frail human beings upon whom too much trust has been placed, "political messiahs" who are bound to fail us as they are in many ways no different to us. It is time we took back power from our "heroes" and vested it in ourselves so we can do something about our current plight instead of waiting for someone, some party, or some organisation to make things better for us. It is time we moved from a focus on "people of power" to a genuine focus on "the power of the people" as highlighted by Luthando Tofu.

Lessons For Africa from 1920s Harlem

This week I revisit one of my favourite eras of history, The Jazz Age, 1920s America. The era that produced that profound piece of literature, The Great Gatsby, by a literary giant, F. Scott Fitzgerald. In the midst of this period of immense historical significance emerged a movement within the confines of Harlem, New York City that was to impact America and shape history in a manner that had multi-generational implications. This movement was initially titled the "New Negro Movement" but eventually became popularised

163

under the label, Harlem Renaissance. This movement holds certain core lessons that are relevant to contemporary Africa in its quest to come out of the doldrums and play a key part in the development of the human race in the twenty-first century.

The Harlem Renaissance was a cultural movement amongst African Americans which emerged in the 1920s in Harlem, a poor neighbourhood of New York City. This movement lasted for a short period between the 1920s and 1930s but the ideas that emerged from it were to live for much longer and impact successive generations of African Americans, American society and even more significantly the "Black" world at large.

The Harlem Renaissance was driven primarily by African Americans, with the support of African American patrons, businesses, and publications. Even though it was in Harlem, New York City, it impacted black scholars and intellectuals from Francophone Africa, France itself, the Caribbean colonies and the English-speaking colonies of Africa. It was a literary and intellectual awakening that promoted and fostered a new black cultural identity that was rooted in the philosophical concept of "The New Negro." It was believed that this "New Negro" could, through intellect and the production of works of art, music, literature etc. challenge existing stereotypes and promote a progressive political agenda and social integration. In this period African American-owned literature and publications flourished, freeing African Americans from the control of mainstream America, which just so happened to be white. Publications such as W.E.B Du Bois's journal, the Crisis, led the way and launched the literary careers of such luminaries as Langston Hughes, Countee Cullen etc. The Harlem Renaissance consisted of various innovations and inventions, with new literary styles, new forms of jazz poetry and new ideologies such as Garveyism emerging.

New intellectuals emerged from within it and it produced great dramatists, novelists, poets, visual artists, musicians, composers, and entertainers. Eminent poets such as Langston Hughes, Clarissa Scott Delany, Lillian Byrnes, Lewis Alexander etc. also emerged during this period of unprecedented cultural awakening. Famous authors such as Alain Locke, Claude McKay etc. came out of this period and great literary works such as Langston Hughes's, Not Without Laughter and Jean Toomer's Cane were written during this period. Ideologies such as Pan-Africanism flourished and became increasingly prominent during this period, and this inspired the "Back to Africa" movement, even the Civil Rights movement of the 1960s could trace its origins to the Harlem Renaissance. It was a period of increased self-determination, group expression, and personal pride for African Americans.

The Renaissance was, however, more than just a literary or artistic movement. It contained within itself the seed of sociological development for African Americans. It redefined the concept of "Blackness" and changed how Americans and the rest of the world looked at African Americans. It produced a greater social consciousness in the African American population and led to African Americans becoming players on the global stage. It led to the intellectual and social development of African Americans.

So, apart from debunking the myth that Maths and Science are the key academic disciplines that are imperative for Africa's development and that the humanities are at best peripheral and at worst insignificant in Africa's quest for development, what relevance, you may ask does this Renaissance hold for contemporary Africa? Firstly, it holds significance for us in its focus on redefinition. We need to redefine the concept of "Africanness" in a manner that is inclusive, conciliatory, and free of the racial and colonial baggage of the past. Just like the Harlem Renaissance was founded on the concept of the "New Negro" we need to ground our quest for development and progress as Africans on the concept of the "New African." This should not be equated to Nietzsche's "Ubermensch" or Che Guevara's impractical "New Socialist Man" ideology. The "New African" philosophy which should undergird our developmental efforts simply implies an African who is: intellectually astute, a pioneer, an innovator, an initiator, confident, forward-looking, unshackled from constant reference to and focused on his colonial past, rooted in his cultural heritage without letting that heritage become a stumbling block to his progress, an ideological leader and a focal point of global civilisation and human progress and development.

Secondly, the Harlem Renaissance holds lessons for contemporary Africa in that it was a cultural awakening that was futuristic, innovative, and progressive. It wasn't intensely focused on re-capturing the negro's past heritage as much as it was on redefining, repositioning, and reworking the negro's culture and re-interpreting it in a modern context. Too often in Africa when we think of cultural awakening, we aim to recapture and relive the culture of our ancestors and predecessors instead of looking to re-interpret that culture to modernise it and move forward. This is an important aspect to consider when looking at cultural awakening because culture by its nature is progressive, not static. It is constantly evolving and changing. Our focus on cultural awakening should profit from our rich past but invest in the present and the future. We should look to move our cultures forward as Africans, instead of holding on to outdated cultural expressions and norms just for the sake of keeping our "group pride."

Thirdly the Harlem Renaissance holds lessons for Africa in its focus on self-determination and ownership. The Harlem Renaissance was driven by African Americans for African Americans. It was sponsored and supported by African American patrons. This is a key lesson for Africa as we pursue the twin goals of growth and development. The developmental agenda for Africa should not be driven by the IMF, the World Bank, The UN, or any other external organisations. It should be driven by Africans for Africans. It should primarily be financed by African finance and financiers before it is financed by the Chinese or any other external sources and where external funding is imperative, we should ensure that the agenda being pushed and promoted in the deals being concluded is primarily an Afro-centric agenda. Africans need to become owners and not just middlemen as we embark on developmental projects on the continent, even where external funding is sourced. This needs to be one of the core conditions that are attached to any financing deals struck with those who come from outside the continent.

Finally, the Harlem Renaissance holds lessons for Africa in its focus on innovation, creativity, and pioneering. During the period of the Harlem Renaissance new literary forms emerged, new forms of jazz and poetry emerged, and a new breed of intellectuals emerged. Africa needs to become the focal point in the battle for ideas in the twenty-first century. New paradigms need to emerge from Africa, new economic systems, new ideas on how to organise and structure society politically, and new intellectuals need to emerge who are not bound by the limitations of colonialism and who aren't focussed on apportioning blame for Africa's woes, but rather coming up with fresh, innovative, relevant solutions for the continent's multi-faceted problems. Creative business ideas and solutions need to emerge to solve the unemployment problem that pervades the entire continent. Africa needs new strategies, philosophies, cultural expressions, policies, and ideologies to emerge that will not only put the continent on the front foot but will leave a multi-generational legacy that will positively impact future generations, as the Harlem Renaissance did when it influenced the Civil Rights generation in America to present-day America where the sitting president is a direct beneficiary of this rich legacy. The Harlem Renaissance also holds lessons for contemporary Africa in the way it embraced modernity and used the benefits of modernity to work at improving the plight of African Americans. Instead of looking at modernity as a "European" concept and a threat to Africa's rich cultural heritage, contemporary Africa needs to embrace modernity and use its many developments and benefits to improve the plight of the African people.

I end off with the poignant words of one Robert Mangaliso Sobukwe, uttered in a speech he gave in his final year as a student at Fort Hare University, "The old order is changing, ushering in a new order. The great revolution has started, and Africa is the field of operation. We have made our choice and have chosen African Nationalism because of its deep human significance; because of its inevitability and necessity to world progress.... It is necessary for human progress that Africa be fully developed and only the Africans can do so. We want to build a New Africa and only we can build it. The opponents of African Nationalism, therefore, are hampering the progress and development not only of Africa but of the whole world." It is, "time for Africa."

Centres Of Intellection

I recently read about an initiative which I believe is of strategic significance to the future of the continent, pioneered by former Director General in the Presidency in South Africa, Joel Netshitenzhe, a man of sharp intellect whose contribution to South Africa and Africa's cause has been greatly undervalued in my books.

The initiative I am talking about is The Mapungubwe Institute for Strategic Reflection (MISTRA), where a group of African intellectuals will come together to develop, contest and pioneer ideas to make a significant contribution in terms of solving the problems of Africa and the world.

This initiative is of extreme significance because one of the things that we need to do as Africans, to make our contribution to the quest for human growth and development in the 21st century, is to take the lead in the formation, development and articulation of ideas. As William Raeper and Linda Smith, authors of a book I have just read recently titled, A Brief Guide to Ideas says, "Ideas are very important. Behind conversations, media, television, political opinions, and educational policy there are often whole philosophies which go unnoticed because people have never learned to think about things in this way. If your mind can learn to travel over different territories of thought, it will be a source of interest and challenge to you all your life. And amid so many opinions, beliefs, values, and changes in our society today, you may be able to learn to recognise what is really being said- where the ideas come from and where they lead to."

Africa needs more Institutes of Strategic Reflection, like the one pioneered by Netshitenzhe. We need to have Centres of Intellection all over the continent, where African intellectuals can come together to debate and discuss ideas and the current issues of the day, with no pressure for immediate results but simply with a mandate to put Africa at the forefront of the formation and development of ideas in our century.

This is similar to what the Ancient Greeks used to do and as a result, they have had an incalculable influence on Western civilisation and by default the rest of the world and how we think about the world. The Ancient Greeks invented mathematics, science, and philosophy. They were the first people to set down proper history and they thought about the world in an open-minded way, free from set ideas given by any belief system.

Alongside philosophy, the Greeks produced great literature with Homer's Iliad and Odyssey, great drama with the tragedies of Sophocles, Euripides, and Aeschylus and great architecture. Greece itself was divided into warring states, among the most important of which were Athens and Sparta. These city-states had differing forms of government: some were democracies, some were ruled by an aristocracy, and some were subject to a tyrant. The Greeks stand at the very beginning of our search for knowledge about the world. How they thought still influences how we think and how we structure and order our societies today.

Similar to Ancient Greece, Africa consists of many nation-states, many of which are involved in wars of all kinds. Amongst these nation-states, some, like South Africa are more important than others in terms of power and influence, just like we found with the Greek city-states. Just like the Greek city-states, African states are characterised by differing forms of government: some are democracies, some are still ruled by monarchs, and some are unfortunately ruled by tyrants. Amid all these realities and challenges, none of which were uncommon to the Greek city-states, Africa can lead the world in the realm of ideas in the 21st century if we prioritise the creation and cultivation of these Centres of Intellection. With this in mind, I hope that the Mapungubwe Institute for Strategic Reflection will inspire other African nations to create their own Centres of Intellection and put the continent at the forefront of world development in this century.

Africa's Need for a Renaissance And Reformation Of Carolingian Proportions

During the first half of this year as part of my academic programme, I enrolled for a course titled: Advanced African Philosophy. This course served as an eye-opener for me as I was exposed to the works of great African scholars such as Kwasi Wiredu, Ngugi wa Thiongo, Wole Soyinka, Leopold Senghor etc. This course was not only intellectually challenging and stimulating but it awakened in me a desire to see Africa having its own Carolingian Renaissance.

The Carolingian Renaissance was a period of intellectual and cultural revival in Europe from the late 8th century until the 9th century. In this period in Europe; education, literature, law, theology, architecture, art, and music all flourished. This Renaissance had a spectacular effect on education and culture in Europe. The chief architects of this Renaissance were the Carolingian ruler Charlemagne and the English monk Alcuin.

During this period there was a sense of renewal in newly stabilised European society galvanised by an elite group of scholars gathered at the court of Charlemagne. In the court of Charlemagne, the people displayed a love of knowledge for its own sake. In the Carolingian Empire as a whole, the skills of reading and writing were not only the keys to faith but to knowledge and power as well. This is exactly the kind of Renaissance that Africa needs to undergo if we are going to achieve all our developmental objectives and turn the continent around.

This is important because modernity will require that Africans acquire a set of new skills, disciplines, ethics, and attitudes. It is also significant because Africa will need intellectual, institutional, administrative, financial, and political synergy to bring about change and improve the lot of its people. The difficulty we have at the moment is that in the process of following the goals of growth, development, and modernisation, Africa has given in to the disease of pragmatism and end-product-focused learning instead of fostering the Carolingian attitude of loving knowledge for its own sake, chiefly because our focus has just been on increasing production and productivity so we can create more jobs and employ more people. The education system and educational institutions across Africa are concentrating on producing employable graduates who can make an immediate impact on the gross domestic product of a nation instead of the Carolingian focus on developing intellectuals who can come up with new concepts, ideas, systems, structures, and strategies that will benefit society in the long term. The focus has moved away from those academic disciplines that stimulate thinking, lead to the introduction of new ideas and revolutionise society to those that make people immediately economically productive.

This becomes counter-productive in the long term as highlighted by the French intellectual Albert Camus when he said that, "the society based on production is only productive, not creative." So, our focus on using education to increase production and productivity is hindering our progress because it produces university graduates who are employees and not necessarily thinkers, intellectuals, and pioneers who can challenge accepted norms and introduce new ideas that will take society much further in the long term. This is a hindrance because whilst the focus on immediate results and production produces gradual change, new ideas have the ability to revolutionise a society to the extent of taking it forward by a whole generation compared to where society was before the new idea was introduced.

Africa needs to focus on producing intellectuals much more than it needs to focus on producing economically active citizens because as Blaise Pascal said, "the greater intellect one has, the more originality one finds in men" and Africa is dying for dynamic, new, original solutions to age-old problems. The irony is that a more intellectual society will in the long term produce much more in a shorter span than a merely pragmatic society that is geared towards producing graduates who are not necessarily thinkers and intellectuals, but employees prepared for their vocation by higher education. This is so because a creative society, based on a foundation of intellectualism, will stem forth entrepreneurs who will create new products or introduce revolutionary ideas that will lead to the establishment of new enterprises that create jobs and grow the gross domestic product of a country.

Most African societies are plagued by the lack of an intellectual culture amongst their populaces, even amongst the educated classes who may be highly qualified but not necessarily intellectuals and thinkers. As Martin Heidegger, the German philosopher once said, "The most thought-provoking thing in our time is that we are still not thinking." Yet how can we when the pursuit of profit, the constant deadlines, meetings, and all kinds of economic objectives make it well-nigh impossible for us as individuals and consequently as a society to value intellectualism and thinking for its own sake? The system as a whole is in some way "anti-intellectual" because it just makes us economically active and productive citizens who are not necessarily intellectual even when we are highly educated. That is why the Greek philosopher Aristotle stated that "all paid jobs absorb and degrade the mind." You get so focused on just doing your job and meeting deadlines that you don't have much time to develop your intellect. This makes society develop much more slowly in the long term.

Africa's developmental challenges require new approaches and new ideas. The old ideas and strategies have not worked for the continent. This requires that Africa's educational institutions focus on producing a different kind of graduate, a graduate who has a love for knowledge for its own sake instead of graduates who look at education purely from the perspective of improving their income-earning ability in future.

The French philosopher Simone de Beauvoir said that "the writer of originality, unless dead is always shocking, scandalous and novel, which disturbs and repels people." Such a man was Charles Darwin, and his ideas still influence the world today, such a man was Karl Marx, and his ideas still influence the world today, such a man was John Maynard Keynes, and his ideas still influence the world today, such a man was Adam Smith, and his ideas still influence the world today. Where are Africa's future Darwin's, Marx's, Keynes', Smith's, and so on? Are our educational institutions producing this calibre of graduates with such depth of intellect? Has pragmatism become so dominant that intellectualism has been relegated to the background? We would do well to heed the words of the philosopher Hegel, "Mark this well, you proud men of action! You are, after all, nothing but unconscious instruments of the men of thought." Where are the men and the women of thought in Africa today?

The American poet, Ralph Waldo Emerson said that "a chief event in life is the day in which we have encountered a mind that startled us." Where are the African minds and intellects that startle us? Africa desperately needs its own Carolingian Renaissance to produce this calibre of individuals. Two particular groups of people could act as the catalyst for this kind of Renaissance: The African university student and the African middle class. Just like Charlemagne's court of scholarly elites galvanised Europe into an intellectual and cultural renaissance dubbed the Carolingian Renaissance, Africa's university campuses and middle-class hang-out spots could become the "court of scholars" that takes Africa into an intellectual and cultural renaissance that will lead to development, growth, and modernisation in the long term.

Our universities need to be transformed from being simple production lines for employers to being intellectual and cultural seedbeds that produce an African intelligentsia capable of producing fresh ideas, new concepts, and ground-breaking inventions and innovations. Our universities need to start producing graduates who can put Africa at the forefront of the world of ideas and hence at the forefront of civilisation. Our universities need to be capable of leading Africa not just into a cultural and intellectual renaissance but also into a reformation like the Reformation that Europe went through under the influence of the likes of Martin Luther, John Calvin, and Ulrich Zwingli. It is important that we not just have a renaissance but a reformation through our universities for various reasons. In the ancient Greek world education and the pursuit of knowledge had as its end goal the pursuit of a good and virtuous life. In the modern world, the pursuit of knowledge and education has as its end goal the pursuit of a more affluent life in a material sense. So, education has gone from being geared towards producing better people in the ancient world to being focused on increasing people's income-earning potential in the modern world so that they can live a more affluent life. Given that one of Africa's biggest problems is corruption and greed, an education system that only produces graduates who are capable of earning more and producing more is not going to suffice. We need an education system that will also focus on producing more virtuous graduates. This is the only long-term solution to corruption in Africa. To quote the Greek philosopher Plato, "knowledge becomes evil if the aim is not virtuous." The people, who have destroyed Africa the most post-independence, are Western-educated intellectual elites because the system under which they were educated did not necessarily value or prioritise virtue as an end goal of academic endeavour.

It was a problem also identified by the French philosopher Michel de Montaigne, "we only labour to stuff the memory, and leave the conscience and the understanding unfurnished and void." Hence the need for a reformation as well as a renaissance because the Reformation in Europe was an intellectual as well as a moral revolution, with the leading Reformers all being scholars of the first order, who had mastery over ideas, logic, language, and texts of classical thought and medieval scholasticism. Africa needs an intellectual as well as a moral revolution hence the need for a renaissance as well as a reformation. Another reason why there is a need for a reformation as well as a renaissance is the fact that if you look at the Reformation in Europe most of their leaders were well versed in diverse works. Martin Luther for example was well versed in works ranging from Aristotle to Seneca, Augustine to Peter Lombard. In other words, they were not necessarily specialised scholars as we find in the modern sense. The Industrial Revolution and capitalism have turned us all into specialists to the detriment of our intellectual development. We study and specialise in a particular field just so we can increase our income-earning potential which probably makes us more productive but hampers our development intellectually. The African university needs to be a "scholarly court" that produces intellectuals with the width and breadth of knowledge that was characteristic of Reformers like Luther.

The Reformation in Europe was also a revolution in ideas and institutions. Africa is in desperate need of an institutional revolution and the formulation of new institutions that will take it towards its developmental goals as at present some of the institutions that we have inherited from European thought have not necessarily been effective in the African context. Can we create new institutions tailor-made for the African landscape? This is another reason why we need to have a reformation as well as a renaissance.

Finally, the African middle class needs to become an intellectual class of revolutionary impact and not just an economically productive class. Here I will appeal to the words of Frantz Fanon, "what I call middle-class is any society that becomes rigidified in pre-determined forms, forbidding all evolution, all gains, all progress, and all discovery. I call the middle class a closed society, in which life has no taste, in which the air is tainted, and in which ideas and men are corrupt. And I think that a man who takes a stand against this death is in a sense a revolutionary." Africa's middle class is too often characterised by these traits identified by Frantz Fanon. It is a middle class that rarely contributes new ideas, rarely challenges the status quo, is happy to accept things as they are as long as it is benefitting as a class no matter what decay

175

society is in, is often driven by greed and corruption of the vilest kind and contributes very little in terms of genuine intellectual and academic pursuits. Just like the African student, the African middle class also needs to act as the catalyst for a revolution of Carolingian proportions and impact in Africa.

So, there is a clear challenge for the African student and the African middle class; will you take up the call to lead the continent into a renaissance of Carolingian proportions and a reformation of similar impact to the European Reformation or will you continue to live selfishly, focus on personal advancement, self-promotion, and material self-interest? Will you lead Africa into a cultural, intellectual, and moral revolution so that the continent can maximise its potential and meet all its developmental objectives? Remember the words of Steve Bantu Biko, "In order to achieve real action you must yourself be a living part of Africa and of her thought, you must be an element of that popular energy which is entirely called forth for the freeing, the progress and the happiness of Africa. There is no place outside that fight for the artist or for the intellectual who is not himself concerned with, and completely at one with the people in the great battle of Africa and of suffering humanity."

A Thinking Society

I have always thought that one of the biggest weaknesses in African society has been our inability to build a "thinking culture." What made the ancient civilisations of Rome and Greece so influential to the extent that a lot of their ideas still influence the world today in terms of how society is ordered and structured, was the fact that they cultivated a culture of thinking, which led to the emergence of ground-breaking new ideas and inventions.

It was William Blake who said that "the sleep of reason begets monsters" and a close look at contemporary African society proves this statement to be true. Our public discourse is shallow and simplistic owing to the lack of a thinking culture. Our political leadership lacks imagination and creativity in tackling some of our socio-economic challenges owing to the lack of development of a thinking culture.

Albert Camus said "We get into the habit of living before acquiring the habit of thinking. In that race which daily hastens us towards death, the body maintains its irreparable lead." This statement accurately depicts our contemporary reality and is a large part of the reason why the continent remains behind other continents in the areas of innovation and invention, all necessary tools for progress and development. It is of fundamental importance that we cultivate a culture of thinking amongst our people if Africa's massive potential is ever going to be fully realised. In the words of Blaise Pascal, "The greater intellect one has, the more originality one finds in men." A society of thinking individuals will always outperform a society of pragmatists in the long term and as such we need to place much more value on the activity of thinking and intellection than we currently do if we are serious about seeing a turnaround on the continent.

Of course, creating a culture of thinking entails more than just formal education. Too often one of the great weaknesses of education systems in Africa has been that they are more focused on teaching people what to think than how to think. We have graduates whose capacity to think originally, argue and articulate in the most compelling and cogent manner as well as use reason to settle social issues is highly underdeveloped because all they have been taught through the formal education system is how to memorise and parrot already existing paradigms and norms. This stifles innovation and keeps us from finding creative solutions for Africa's many problems.

The shortage of a thinking culture can often be seen in how we engage in and settle public disputes. People often resort to labelling to settle disputes but as the Cuban revolutionary Ernesto "Che" Guevara put it, "a label is not an argument." We ostracise and marginalise those who dare to disagree with us. In the words of Bertrand Russell, "If you think that your belief is based upon reason, you will support it by argument, rather than by persecution and will abandon it if the argument goes against you." This is an area of great weakness amongst Africans and often means that we speak past each other whenever having a supposed debate on issues that are of public importance. We find it easier to gravitate towards ad hominem, ad baculum, and ad populum arguments and we fall prey to the phenomenon identified by the French philosopher Michel de Montagne, "he who establishes his argument by noise and command shows that his reason is weak."

It is often quite humorous to see the level to which our debates often degenerate in different public forums and is a clear indicator of a need for the cultivation of a 'thinking culture." Another mistake we often make is to mistake thinking or intellectual discourse for agreement or disagreement. People often enter discussions and debates with the single intention of getting people to agree with them, instead of testing the soundness of their beliefs and ideologies as well as enriching themselves by learning from the other person, whether there is a final agreement or not. As the poet Robert Frost put it, "Thinking isn't agreeing or disagreeing. That's voting."

Another hindrance to the development of a thinking culture is that our education system is geared towards producing human beings who are employable instead of giving them the tools to acquire knowledge and contribute new ideas and concepts in the realm of knowledge production. In the words of the American poet Ezra Pound, "Real education must ultimately be limited to men who insist on knowing, the rest is mere sheepherding." In other words, an education system must be based on a culture of knowing, of curiosity, of wanting to know and discover things. Until we have citizens with this kind of attitude all we will be doing is "sheepherding" and it's a small wonder that we'll continue to be a society of people who can't do much for themselves, because that is the nature of sheep. They rely completely on the shepherd.

The German philosopher Martin Heidegger's words are unfortunately an accurate description of much of African society, "the most thought-provoking thing in our thought-provoking time is that we are still not thinking." We need to build societies made up of thinking citizens if we are going to see the continent grow, develop, and progress as much as we'd like it to. We need to value thinking for thinking's sake, and this will be seen in the amounts African societies at all levels invest in things like research and development. We need to remember the German philosopher Georg Wilhelm Friedrich Hegel's injunction, "Mark this well, you proud men of action! You are, after all, nothing but unconscious instruments of the men of thought." If Africa wants to start leading instead of following, we need to build thinking societies made up of thinking citizens.

Institutions Not Individuals

With all the talk in the past few weeks being about the Middle East and the apparent push for democratisation in that region, comparable to that which happened in Eastern Europe after the fall of the Berlin wall in 1989, I found myself thinking about the continent of Africa and its levels of democratisation.

Political scientists will tell us that Africa had its moment of democratisation in the 1990s with many African countries having embraced "democracy" and having held their first "free and fair" elections with multi-party structures for the first time in this period. However, the push for democratisation on the continent seems to have run out of steam in the 2000s with many leaders refusing to relinquish power after having lost elections, to the point of questioning the validity of these election results in the first place.

The question that needs to be asked is whether the democratisation of Africa in the 1990s was ever genuine in the first place since it has failed to rid the continent of autocratic governments, dictatorial leaders, and despots. It would appear that we have made the fundamental mistake of confusing electoralism and multi-partyism with democratisation and the entrenchment of a democratic culture. The holding of periodic elections contested by a multiplicity of political parties and individuals does not constitute the democratisation of a society.

In Africa, we have seen many sham elections being held, with ruling parties which have governed for decades and have entrenched themselves and their hegemony at every level of society, and opposition parties which have no realistic chance of ever winning elections. Apart from questioning the validity of most of these elections, where ruling parties often don't play fair and leave very little room for opposition parties to campaign and contest elections in an environment free of intimidation and fear, one has to say that the fact that we have seen so many elections in Africa where a multiplicity of political parties contested elections and yet only one party (often the ruling party) has a realistic chance of winning, brings into question whether what we have experienced in Africa is indeed democratisation.

Barring a few exceptions, we have seen many "democratic elections" on the continent which have returned liberation-era leaders and political parties into power with big victory margins which indicate that the opposition never really had a realistic chance of winning in the first place. This often happens because the average African citizen still holds liberation-era political parties and political leaders in higher esteem than the democratic institutions and structures that have been put in place to try and instil a democratic culture in African societies. It is only when the average citizen holds the democratic institutions and structures that have been set in place in higher regard than their favourite political leaders and political affiliations that we can say that true democratisation has occurred. This is what societies like America have gotten right. Whether the average American is a Democrat or a Republican, they respect their institutions much more than their political organisations and leaders and would never allow their leaders and parties to undermine and denigrate those institutions under any circumstances. The average African citizen however still places more confidence in political leaders and political organisations than in the democratic institutions that have been put in place in society.

Even in a society that has a highly revered constitution like South Africa and well-developed democratic institutions in place, the primary loyalty of the South African citizen is not to the constitution and our democratic institutions but to political parties and political leaders, a clear indication that democratisation has not yet taken place contrary to popular belief. This is highly unfortunate because democratic institutions are more reliable than individual political leaders, no matter how morally upright and principled they are. For example, in a century (20th century) that produced two of the greatest moral political leaders the world has ever known, Nelson Mandela and Mahatma Gandhi (ok three if you include Martin Luther King Jr), we still had the likes of Pol Pot, Josef Stalin, Adolf Hitler, Idi Amin, Mao Tse-Tung, Joseph Mobutu, Sukarno, Suharto etc.

In other words, for every great moral political leader like Nelson Mandela, you have two or three Hitlers and Stalins. So, when we look at the construction of society, we should construct our societies expecting Hitlers and Stalins instead of Gandhis and Mandelas. Gandhis and Mandelas are the exception in political leadership. Hitlers and Stalins (or milder, more moderate variants of them) are the norm and hence it is folly to place so much confidence in individual political leaders. This is the curse of Africa. When we have truly democratised, we will be in a place where we trust institutions more than individuals. Even in a society that has been blessed with a Mandela, there is no guarantee that the leaders that come after him will be of the same ilk, as has been evidenced in contemporary South Africa and as such it is folly to trust individuals and political organisations more than democratic institutions.

Another clear indicator of democratisation on the continent will be the creation of viable opposition parties with a clear chance of winning elections. As long as the political opposition parties in Africa contest elections without any realistic chance of winning elections, we will continue to have electoralism and multi-partyism without genuine democracy. Africa is still awaiting its moment of democratisation when the average African citizen will place more confidence in democratic institutions than individuals and there will be elections that are contested in a free and fair manner with different political parties having a realistic chance of winning these elections instead of just the one, which is what we are seeing now. It is time we focussed on inculcating a culture of respect for democracy and democratic institutions amongst African people to truly democratise.

5

Pertinent Affairs

So Much for The African Solution

A big story that has made headlines over the past week has been the story of the Ivory Coast presidential elections and the political deadlock that has resulted in that country because of it. Incumbent president Laurent Gbagbo, after clearly losing the presidential run-off election to his opponent, Alassane Ouattara, decided not to accept the outcome and hence not to concede defeat. After the electoral commission had declared Ouattara to be the rightful winner of the election, the pro-Gbagbo constitutional council reversed the provisional results illegally and declared Gbagbo to be the winner. The UN, the US, EU, AU, France, and ECOWAS have called for Gbagbo to accept the election results and step down. He has refused, got himself "inaugurated" and we are now faced with the ridiculous situation where both men are claiming to be the legitimate president of the Ivory Coast.

Naturally, violence has broken out in the country with supporters of both men vowing to do whatever it takes to see their man being instilled as Ivory Coast president. Amid all this, a familiar sight emerged, that of former South African president Thabo Mbeki, going to the Ivory Coast with an AU mandate to mediate between the two parties hoping to evade violence and resolve the issue in an amicable, peaceful manner. Seeing all this play out left one with a certain sense of déjà vu. We have seen all of this play out all too often in the recent past in Africa. Remember Zimbabwe: Robert Mugabe, Morgan Tsvangirai, Arthur Mutambara, and the "Global

Political Agreement" that ushered in a "unity" government to avoid violence once Mugabe and ZANU-PF refused to accept that they had lost an election and hence the legitimate right to power? Remember Mwai Kibaki, Raila Odinga and the unity government that was formed in Kenya after violence had broken out when Kibaki refused to accept that he had lost an election? All these unity governments were celebrated as victories for the much-celebrated "African solutions for African problems" approach and as a sign of maturity and a coming of age for African politics and politicians.

However, this seems to have started and encouraged a trend where African leaders who have lost an election can refuse to accept the result, mobilise their supporters in a campaign of violence and intimidation and hope that the other party will eventually be willing to compromise so that they can maintain some, if not all of their hold on power, even if it is by illegitimate means. This is clearly the card that Laurent Gbagbo is playing in this situation and since a precedent has been set, it's going to be very difficult for a different solution to be found for this impasse. It's time that we as Africans stand up and end this culture of "political agreements" and "unity" governments that are undemocratic and a betrayal of the people's wishes. The only way to do that is for the AU to insist and ensure that Laurent Gbagbo steps down from power and allows Alassane Ouattara to take over the reins as Ivory Coast's legitimately elected president. Anything else would be a blatant betrayal of democratic principles and an encouragement to other African leaders to follow the same approach when faced with electoral defeat.

Multiculturalism, Nationalism and Pan-Africanism

A recent statement by German Chancellor Angela Merkel that, "multiculturalism has failed in Germany" caused a lot of controversy and got me thinking about the concepts of multiculturalism, nationalism, and Pan-Africanism. In a globalised world that is increasingly interconnected and interdependent, the twenty-first century was supposed to usher in an unprecedented period of cultural, ethnic, and racial tolerance with traditional boundaries being done away with and the free flow of goods and human capital between countries being promoted.

We have seen moves for greater unity and cooperation in the different regions of the world with the European Union and the mooted African Union being primary examples of this "New World Order" where different countries would band together to create stronger economic blocs with traditional geographic boundaries being of secondary significance. This would be founded on greater solidarity and cooperation amongst people of different ethnicities, cultures, and races. Germany with its frontline role in the push for European unity and its diverse, multicultural society, with immigrants from Eastern Europe and countries such as Turkey was supposed to be a shining example of this "new way" of operating and relating in the twenty-first century. So, when Chancellor Merkel categorically states that "multiculturalism has failed in Germany" it raises a lot of questions about where the world is going in the new century.

Chancellor Merkel's statement simply expressed a sentiment that most Germans agree with and revealed a trend that has become increasingly common in Europe as a rising nationalism in the different Eurozone countries threatens to roll back the hard-earned work that has been put in to create a strong, united Europe. Ordinary German citizens, facing economic hardships and uncertainties have become increasingly agitated with immigrants from other countries who they claim take away economic opportunities from them and are an unnecessary burden on German society. This is a phenomenon that has been witnessed in different countries such as Russia, France and even Britain which is changing its immigration laws to cut down on the number of immigrants that come into that country on an annual basis. So, is the world going to be dominated by strong, united political and economic blocs like the EU and the AU with more open flows of goods, services, and human capital between these countries or will the rising nationalism, ethnic consciousness and battle for resources take us back to the era of independent, sovereign nation-states? What does that mean for Africa and its push for an African Union and the ideal of Pan-Africanism?

These are all questions that I began to ask myself as I pondered Chancellor Merkel's statement. In an African continent where different ethnic groups in individual countries are battling to get along and to work together to create successful, prosperous nation-states, is it realistic to expect the whole continent to cooperate and work together to create a strong, unified African Union based on the ideal of Pan Africanism? Is Pan-Africanism even genuine? At a time when Sudan is considering splitting up because of ethnic and religious tensions, Somaliland is looking for its own independence, the Buganda tribe is looking for greater autonomy in Uganda and there are secessionist movements and ethnic tensions right across the continent, is it not naïve to be promoting Pan Africanism when Africans are battling to get along even within their individual states?

I began to question Pan-Africanism as an ideology. Does this Pan-African attitude even exist amongst ordinary Africans? I remembered a story that a friend of mine recently told me which caused me to doubt and question -Pan-Africanism even more. My friend who is Ghanaian-South African was raised in South Africa, went to South African schools and received his higher education in South Africa and now works in South Africa. His family moved to South Africa many years ago, became South African citizens and have raised their children as South Africans, but when my friend developed a romantic interest in a South African girl of Zulu heritage, the family made it clear that it would be unacceptable for him to marry a South African lass and instead preferred that he marry a woman of Ghanaian heritage. For them this was non-negotiable. So, my friend was faced with a choice: either marry the South African girl and rebel against his family or let go of the relationship and find a Ghanaian girl. A Ugandan-South African friend of mine also told me how his family and the Ugandan-South

African community that he grew up in also held similar attitudes and often showed condescending attitudes towards black South Africans even though they had lived in South Africa for a long time and raised their children as South Africans. These kinds of attitudes can be found all around the continent, with different ethnic groups and tribal factions betraying similar attitudes and, in my books, this calls into question the concept of Pan-Africanism. Maybe we have deceived ourselves into believing that Africans are for one another when the reality on the ground is that we battle to get along with and respect each other in our tribal groups within the different countries.

If that is so why is Pan-Africanism so favoured by African intellectuals and academics? If different ethnic groups are battling to unite and work together to build successful countries in the individual states how realistic is it to hold Nkrumahist expectations of a united, prosperous Africa? It could just be that nationalism, ethnicism, and tribalism will derail all these grandiose unity and cooperation plans because that seems to be the default nature of not just Africans, but humans right across the spectrum as evidenced by the fledgling European Union. With all this in mind, the question that I couldn't answer was: what does that mean for Africa and the world in the twenty-first century? Will it be greater cooperation, unity, solidarity, and interdependence based on the reality of globalisation or will the greater forces of nationalism and ethnicism prevail and leave us with a world of fiercely independent, proud nation-states that battle to cooperate and compete aggressively with each other in the battle to improve the quality of life and the standards of living of their particular citizens? Maybe Arthur Schopenhauer was right in stating that, "national character is only another name for the particular form which the littleness, perversity and baseness of mankind take in every country. Every nation mocks at other nations, and all are right."

Osama Bin Laden And The Death Of Terrorism

It is now common knowledge that the United States of America finally captured and killed Osama Bin Laden after a search that lasted almost a decade, spread across many nations and cost tens of thousands of lives. Of course, the death of Bin Laden leaves us with many unanswered questions, one of which is whether his death will truly reduce the threat of terrorism around the world as we have been led to believe.

In my view, the death of Bin Laden is not the most important event in the fight against terrorism that has occurred this year, despite what Barack Obama and the United States would like us to believe. For a long time now, Bin Laden has been nothing but a figurehead for terrorism, with no clear capacity to attack and hurt the United States and its allies. Post-September 11, Bin Laden has been on the run and has shown no real ability to launch an attack of similar proportions.

The most important event that has occurred in the fight against terrorism this year has been the North African and Middle East uprisings, which have come about because Arab civilians who have been under US-sponsored/supported tyrannical leadership for decades, have finally found their voice and are demanding that their rights be respected and that their nations democratise. This is significant because the creation of open Arab societies with renewed respect for the rights of Arab citizens will take away the ability of people like Bin Laden to mobilise young Arab citizens to take up arms and sacrifice their lives under the banner of fighting against so-called American imperialism in the Middle East.

The push for democratisation in the Middle East is of much greater significance in the battle against terrorism than the death of Osama Bin Laden. This is what we need to give greater attention to rather than this sensationalist excitement over the death of a man who undoubtedly had it coming, because as the cliché goes, "if you live by the sword, you will die by the sword." Like all lovers of freedom around the world I am happy that a man who was responsible for the taking of so many innocent lives finally got his comeuppance. However, I do have many other questions that I believe need answering. As a friend of mine said recently in a rather humorous manner, "The Americans spent over a decade, billions of American dollars and killed tens of thousands of people to finally bring Bin Laden to justice only to find that he had been staying at his house in an upper market suburb all along." This leads one to ask the following questions: the victims of September 11 and their families who suffered under Bin Laden's cruelty finally got the justice they have been asking for in the death of Bin Laden, but who will bring justice to the innocent civilians of Afghanistan, Pakistan and other countries who died as "collateral damage" in the US's search for Bin Laden? Bin Laden was responsible for the killing of at least three thousand people on September 11 and for that, he has been rightly killed, but who will bring George W. Bush, Dick Cheney, Donald Rumsfeld, Barack Obama et al to justice for the killing of tens of thousands of innocent people, in the quest to bring Bin Laden down?

Does the world have different standards of justice for different parts of the world depending on how powerful and important certain people and places are? Are the lives of poor, innocent Afghans and Pakistanis not as important as the lives of those who were killed on September 11? If they are equally important, then why isn't there a similar cry for justice to account for these innocent deaths? Just as an extra: exactly who is it who trained, supported and armed Osama Bin Laden and Saddam Hussein in the first place? What was that you said about "state-sponsored" terrorism again?

At The Risk Of Being Accused Of Whataboutism, Western Hypocrisy About The Fifa World Cup In Qatar Is Sickening

Listening to the negative commentary and sentiment about the FIFA World Cup in Qatar, mainly emanating from Western Europe, has been an interesting exercise in affirming the power of historical revisionism, especially in serving the interests of those who find themselves on the dominant side of the historical equation.

FIFA president Gianni Infantino, in his admittedly banal and irrational tirade against criticism of the World Cup in Qatar, made a telling comment that bears repeating as we are forced to deal with the self-righteous criticism of the Qatari FIFA World Cup from the West, *"We have been told many, many lessons from some Europeans, from the western world. I think for what we Europeans have been doing the last 3,000 years we should be apologising for the next 3,000 years before starting to give moral lessons to people."*

Crikey mate, bull's eye!!! Talk about the "pot calling the kettle black" to use a cliché, even at the risk of being accused of whataboutism in doing so. A cursory glance at history leads one to ask the pertinent question: do we (and the Qataris) really need a lecture from the West about upholding and respecting the human rights of *"others"* as well as respect for the human lives of the *"others"*?

Even looking at contemporary times and moving away from merely focusing on historical facts, here are a few hard truths that the self-righteous Westerners who are criticising and ridiculing the World Cup in Qatar will not want to acknowledge or perhaps they are conveniently overlooking: the United States of America and its European allies supply nearly two-thirds of all arms that are transferred to the Middle East and these are arms that have been proven to be the tools that are used to fuel even more conflict and bring about more human rights abuses and loss of civilian lives in the region.

Between 2010 and 2019, the United Kingdom (UK) had a combined $125 billion worth of arms exports, with sixty per cent of those being purchased by Middle Eastern countries such as Kuwait, Qatar (go figure okes), Saudi Arabia, Oman, with Qatar for example purchasing Brimstone missiles from the UK. The Middle East made up seventy-seven per cent of the UK's arms exports in 2018 and in 2019 that figure stood at fifty-eight per cent.

These arms supplies have not only played a significant role in perpetuating conflict within the region, leading to the loss of many innocent lives (for example, in Yemen, arms supplied by the UK and the USA through their alliance with Saudi Arabia have led to the killing of hundreds of thousands of innocent civilians), but they have also been instrumental in propping up brutal regimes with no regard for human rights like Saudi Arabia, all of which makes one wonder why all the self-righteous indignation about Qatar and its human rights record, from the arch proponents of human rights abuses and lack of respect for the human lives of *the "others"*, when one looks globally and historically at the West?

So, next time you hear a Westerner telling you how conflicted they are about this World Cup, whether they can indeed watch and enjoy it in good conscience, given what they claim is Qatar's reputation for human rights abuses and lack of respect for the human lives of those labourers who they import from Asia and of course the rights of the LGBTQIA+ community (I am not downplaying nor dismissing the significance of these issues, so we must not make the classic mistake of tackling a both/and issue with an either/or mindset here), remind them of these poignant words from the twentieth-century American political philosopher, Reinhold Niebuhr in his book, **Moral Man and Immoral Society: A Study in Ethics and Politics**, *"The moral attitudes of dominant and privileged groups are characterised by universal self-deception and hypocrisy. The unconscious and conscious identification of their special interests with general interests and universal values, which we have noted in analysing national attitudes, is equally obvious in the attitude of classes.*

The reason why privileged classes are more hypocritical than underprivileged ones is that special privilege can be defended in terms of the rational ideal of equal justice only, by proving that it contributes something to the good of the whole. Since inequalities of privilege are greater than could possibly be defended rationally, the intelligence of privileged groups is usually applied to the task of inventing specious proofs for the theory that universal values spring from, and that general interests are served by, the special privileges which they hold."

Or, at the risk of sounding like a less enlightened (less erudite too one might add) version of one Archie Mafeje, when one sees all these hypocritical and self-righteous critiques of Qatar from the West, one is left with the question: does the West and do Westerners think that their historically unjust and immoral actions have become constitutionally acceptable and morally justifiable all because of the passage of time, hence their confidence in standing from the rooftop and preaching to the rest of the world about the wrongfulness and immorality of this FIFA World Cup being held in Qatar?

World Economic Forum: What's The Point?

This week an assortment of business executives, university professors, NGO leaders, and political leaders will be gathering in Davos, Switzerland for the 41st World Economic Forum summit. The slogan of the Forum is, "committed to improving the state of the world." Now this is a very noble objective indeed, but it is questionable whether the WEF has managed to contribute anything of substance in its 41 years of existence that has improved the state of the world.

According to the New York Times, a recent WEF Global Risk Report identified 37 major problems facing the world, one more than in 2010. The Forum aims to tackle some of these problems and provide workable solutions that can benefit all of humanity but in reality, very little has come out of these annual meetings of the global elite that has significantly made the world a better place. Klaus Schwab, the founder and executive chairman of the WEF said that he is, "concerned that governments and international organisations can no longer cope with the capacity and fast pace of the new realities of the world we live in."

In light of these new realities, it is sad that the WEF has become nothing more than a talk shop for the rich and powerful, mixed with lots of partying and entertainment. Very little that is discussed at the Forum leads to action that improves the lot of the average person in the world and instead of being a Forum that produces solutions for the world's problems, the WEF has become nothing but an annual retreat for networking and concluding big business deals that only benefit an elite minority.

All the expenditure that goes into organising and hosting this event could be better spent on more worthy causes that contribute positively and improve the world that we live in. When the world was in the depths of an economic crisis last year, the WEF failed to produce anything of substance that could improve the world economy and take us out of recession. It ended up being just an expensive talk shop that neither produced solutions to the challenges that the world was faced with at the time nor anticipated future problems to better prepare us to respond more appropriately and more efficiently.

The world seems to be obsessed with these summits and conferences of the "greatest minds" of our time which end up producing nothing of substance that takes the human race forward and makes the world a better place. We have academic conferences, UN summits, G8 and G20 summits, EU summits and AU summits, and multilateral organisations with all kinds of experts and research groups and yet the world is more unequal than ever before, more people are living in poverty than ever before, socio-economic challenges are increasing and the great political conflicts of the world remain unresolved. It leaves one wondering whether there is indeed any point in convening summits like the World Economic Forum because there is no greater benefit to humanity despite the large amounts of money and effort that go into making them happen.

It's about time that we put an end to these elite gatherings that are just a complete waste of time and money and create new platforms that are going to make a meaningful and significant contribution that will make the world a better place. I don't see any point in the annual gathering of the world's elite in Davos, do you?

Wikileaks And American Hypocrisy

So, WikiLeaks founder Julian Assange was arrested in London sometime this week. His crime: embarrassing the world's most powerful nation by daring to publish information that exposed the naked hypocrisy of American foreign policy. Since WikiLeaks started publishing these documents detailing secret conversations between US diplomats about various people and subjects covering a plethora of global issues, the website has been the victim of web attacks, been cut off by internet service providers, been accused of being irresponsible and its founder, Julian Assange has been accused of things ranging from "terrorism" to rape. As global citizens, what ought we to make of all these interesting developments?

It strikes one as strange that a country that has positioned itself as the promoter of the gospel of democracy, open society, capitalism, media freedom, government accountability to its citizens etc. is now doing everything to prevent the further publication of information which has at best exposed the US for what it truly is, hypocritical and at worst has caused it untold embarrassment and complicated its diplomatic engagements with the rest of the world. To say that WikiLeaks has jeopardised US National Security interests by releasing all of this "classified" information and to suggest that it is not of public interest is to engage in deception of the vilest kind. Firstly, let's look at some of the information that we have become privy to thanks to WikiLeaks.

We have discovered that the US army deliberately targeted refugee camps for bombing. It would be a brave man who would argue that this is "classified" information that the public has no right to know. We also found out that the US gave money to military men from certain countries so that they could buy arms, to further American interests in those parts of the world. You want to tell me that, that isn't an issue of public interest? We were made aware of the fact that the US was spying on the UN Secretary-General. We also discovered information about American relations in the Middle East, with states such as Yemen and interesting little snippets of information about US opinion of countries such as Russia, Iran, Turkey and their leadership. By virtue of having appointed itself the global custodian of democracy, openness, transparency, accountability, justice, and human rights, the US gave up the right to claim that its diplomatic engagements with the rest of the world are of a secret nature and should be of no interest to Joe Public. The US prides itself on its great credentials and exemplary behaviour as a democratic state, but the publication of the documents by WikiLeaks has exposed all of that as a sham and revealed the vast difference between what the US claims to stand for and what it does in its relations with the rest of the world.

American foreign policy has a direct impact on the world and the quest for peaceful co-existence and co-operation between nations and hence what the US does in its engagement with other states and how it goes about doing that is of direct interest to the global public. To see what WikiLeaks and its founder have had to endure for daring to embarrass the world's most powerful nation is to witness a betrayal of all those values which America claims to be promoting in its engagement with other states. Firstly, after the release of the initial set of documents, WikiLeaks founder Julian Assange was suddenly accused of raping two women in Sweden, a charge which he vehemently denies.

This reminds me of a certain rape case in South Africa which had massive political consequences and led to a change in the political landscape. It is of course now history that there was a strong case of political interference in that case with the one party clearly aiming to eliminate a political opponent by all means necessary, even if it meant abusing state resources and state power. As a South African with this background in mind, it strikes one as too convenient that just after WikiLeaks released the initial documents, Assange was accused of rape in a manner that seeks to discredit and silence him from releasing any further information which could be embarrassing. Independent companies like Amazon were bullied by the US government into breaking off their relationship with WikiLeaks, Swiss authorities closed Assange's bank account without any justification, Mastercard pulled the plug on payments to the website, several countries are either making or actively considering aggressive legal moves against Julian Assange, Assange has been called a "terrorist" and there have been calls for him to be assassinated by prominent American political leaders, who constantly preach to the rest of the world the gospel of democracy, transparency, media freedom, human rights etc.

Now this is astounding and incredible. We have a media organisation and its owner being harangued and harassed for daring to publish information that has embarrassed a government and a country that claims to be the quintessential democracy and none of the famed "defenders of media freedom and human rights" are saying anything. The same people who were writing open letters and signing memorandums against the South African government for trying to introduce a media tribunal and pass a stringent Information Bill through its parliament are now conspicuous by their very loud silence. There was a global consensus that what the SA government was proposing would negatively impact the media and its ability to hold the government accountable but when the US is guilty of something even more sinister suddenly all those voices have gone silent. Does no one see anything wrong with this picture?

If Robert Mugabe and his ZANU-PF government or any other African leader and his government had been using their official power and influence to harass a media organisation and its leader for daring to publish information that was embarrassing to that government, there would be a huge international uproar and those African leaders and governments would be accused of having no regard for media freedom and for abusing their power. Now why is no one saying anything when the US is blatantly doing something of a similar nature? Is media freedom, transparency, open society and accountability only a virtue when it serves US interests? All of this smacks of hypocrisy of the worst kind and leads one to conclude that the US is a country that preaches a gospel which it doesn't at all practice in reality.

Sudan And the Risk of a Failed State

In the last few weeks, there has been great excitement in Africa and other parts of the world about South Sudan's possible secession from Sudan and the creation of a new state on the African continent. The theory goes that because the Southern Sudanese have been so marginalised by their northern counterparts, it would be in the best interests of both parties for the South to secede and for a new country to be birthed that will guarantee better prospects for Southerners. Amidst all the excitement and elation for a continent that is desperate for any kind of good news to counter the negativity that often pervades it, it would appear that the question of the economic viability of a South Sudanese state has been ignored or at best completely overlooked.

Here are some facts that should cause us to be a bit more cautious before we celebrate the probable birthing of a new African nation-state, South Sudan: according to an Oxfam report, the south only has a hundred certified midwives serving a population of roughly 8.2 million. Just one in ten deliveries in the South is attended by a skilled birth attendant, 80% of adults in the South (92% of women) cannot read or write, less than 2% of the children complete their primary education and over half the population do not have access to healthy drinking water.

The south has only 50km of paved roads and more than 90% of its population live on less than $1 a day, with almost half the population living off aid. It is also completely landlocked and even though most if not all the oil in Sudan can be found in the south, the pipes needed to transport the oil run through the north. So, we see here that we are faced with the prospect of the birthing of a nation-state which may not be economically viable, and which would require lots of aid and assistance to avoid becoming yet another of many failed states on the continent.

A friend recently accused me of being an Afro-pessimist when I dared to suggest that we can't celebrate the probable birthing of a new nation-state when it is not exactly clear how this would directly positively affect the ordinary South Sudanese. Of course, because of the perceived injustices perpetuated by the North over many years and the marginalisation of the Christian South by the Muslim North, there will be a populist push towards independence which will be highly supported by the populace, but does secession benefit ordinary people in both the north and the south? Are we not better off finding ways to make a united Sudan work together for the greater benefit of its populace? Is self-determination more important than economic freedom and development?

These are just some of the questions that I have been asking myself amid all the euphoria about the possible independence of South Sudan as I have considered some of the great socio-economic challenges it will have to face on its own, once independence has been attained. Post-colonial African history has taught us a very important lesson about the folly of celebrating independence whilst the issue of economic viability and sustainability has not been sufficiently addressed. I hope we are not failing the people of North and South Sudan by celebrating possible independence at the expense of future economic prospects and potential. We must remember the words of the Argentine poet Ricardo Guttierez, "do not sing victory hymns on the sunless day of the battle." Whilst the rest of the continent and the world celebrate the birthing of a new state, the naked reality will be that the new South Sudanese state will be entering into a battle for its very survival as a state, owing to the socio-economic challenges that it will be faced with, which may be better tackled under the banner of one united Sudan. It also seems odd to me that whilst the general push around the world is for unity, greater cooperation and dependence, we Africans are busy celebrating the probable splitting up of one of our key states. For the sake of the ordinary Sudanese, I hope that history proves me wrong and both Sudans find a way to be economically viable and sustainable.

Is Secularism the New Religion of the 21st Century?

I was watching an Al Jazeera news program with a panel of Middle Eastern and North African experts commenting on the recent wave of protests that have struck the region and what it means for the countries in the region in terms of democratisation. A comment made by one of the experts concerning Egypt and the drawing up of a new constitution in that country piqued my interest and got me thinking again.

The military council which is running Egypt in the interim has mandated a group of constitutional law experts to draw up a new constitution so that free and fair democratic elections can be held as soon as possible. The head of this constitutional group is a judge who is known to hold very strong Islamic convictions and upon hearing this, one of the panellists on the Al Jazeera programme proceeded to express his genuine disappointment that a judge with religious convictions had been appointed to oversee the constitution-making process as he had hoped that they would find a secular judge who would ensure that the new Egyptian constitution would be a secular one with no religious undertones. The other experts seemed to agree that secularism and a secular constitution were the best way forward not just for Egypt but for the region.

This seems to be the accepted paradigm for societies that are modernised/modernising and are seemingly "enlightened." It seems that secularism has become the new religion of the 21st century. There seems to be seeming consensus that the best way for human beings to structure and order society, is to build secular societies that are not heavily influenced by religion and religious convictions. It is assumed that secularism is the best way to ensure that society is constructed in a manner that ensures that everyone's views are respected and no one's views are marginalised.

All this sounds quite good but upon closer inspection, one begins to realise that proponents of secularism are not as tolerant as they would like us to believe. They are seemingly tolerant of all people except for those who hold very strong religious convictions.

Proponents of secularism are highly intolerant of those with fundamentalist Islamic and Christian convictions for example. They seek to rid the world of all such people. In this manner, secularism is like the religion of the twenty-first century. Remember in the past when there was no clear distinction between church and state and anyone who believed anything contrary to what the church and Christianity taught was not only ostracised, persecuted, and marginalised but often faced a death sentence for holding those beliefs. Witness the persecution of Galileo Galilei for example for promoting a view which was contrary to what the church taught in his time or the Spanish Inquisition, where all those who taught and promoted ideas that were contrary to what the church espoused were eliminated. These are all examples of intolerance which characterised the world when the church and the state were inextricably linked.

The same thing often happens in countries that are run under Islamic Sharia law and for this reason, proponents of modernity have tried to move away from religion and religious beliefs when looking at constructing society but in a strange twist of history, it is now the proponents of secularism who are guilty of marginalising those with strong religious convictions. Religion is often ridiculed and made to look outdated, irrelevant, and intolerant by those who strongly believe that society should be secularized. People who hold very strong traditional, religious beliefs are caricatured as unsophisticated simpletons who have not moved on with the times. Secularism is made to appear as the only option for the "reasonable man."

On university campuses and amongst the intellectual elite in most modern/modernising societies there seems to be an unspoken alliance to try and put religion on the periphery of society. This is the same kind of intolerance that we have seen being manifested in societies built on religious principles. Secularism has in some ways become the new intolerant religion of the 21st century, modernised, "enlightened" man. In a world that is truly just, fair, and tolerant even those with deep religious convictions, bordering on fundamentalism should be allowed to express and live out their beliefs without being made to feel Jurassic, outdated and out of sync with the realities of the "modern" world.

Religion: Stumbling Block or Necessary Building Block?

Watching a news broadcast recently, detailing religious tensions in certain parts of the world and the deadly consequences for ordinary citizens of the unnecessary conflicts that arise out of these tensions got me thinking about religion and its relevance for the world and the cause of human progress in the twenty-first century. Former British Prime Minister, Tony Blair in an interview he gave recently said that he "thinks that the issue of the twenty-first century is not a fight over political ideology but over cultural, religious ideology." Should religion be that important to us and if so, why?

Most, if not all religions promote or purport to promote the universal values of peace, love, solidarity, the sacredness of human life and tolerance. However, a look at history and the current reality around the globe shows that instead of promoting these values, religion has often been divisive, polarising, and deadly. Witness the brutal, violent nature of the conflict in Nigeria which has seen the country being divided into north and south, Christian versus Muslim, or the tensions in India between a Hindu majority and minorities such as Muslims and Christians and the tensions in Ireland between Catholics and Protestants which caused the unnecessary deaths of many innocent civilians and has been thankfully resolved with a peace agreement that ushered in a unity government.

Wherever you look, religion seems to produce not unity, peace, and greater solidarity but division, violence, and illogical conflicts. With the rise in religious fundamentalism and its growing influence in places as diverse as Iran, America, Afghanistan, Pakistan, the Middle East area, Sudan etc. one needs to question whether religion itself is not a stumbling block to the quest for human

201

progress. Can humanity progress without religion playing a role? Would a post-religion world be better, united and more peaceful than a world with a multiplicity of religions that cause division and violent conflict? The French intellectual Albert Camus seemed to believe that religion was a fundamental building block for human progress as opposed to a stumbling block hence his statement that, "only a philosophy of eternity, in the world today, would justify non-violence."

The American poet Edgar Allan Poe seemed to disagree with this view however and for him, "all religion is simply evolved out of fraud, fear, greed, imagination, and poetry." In other words, religion is by nature a figment of the imagination and completely deceptive and destructive. A look at the unnecessary conflicts and deaths that have arisen from religious differences would seem to bear this out. Do we need religion to progress? Should religious differences even matter, if we do allow for the necessity of religion or should it just be a case of taking the pragmatic view expressed in the old Italian proverb, "When the chess game is over, the pawns, rooks, kings and queens all go back into the same box."

These are questions that need to be answered if we are going to see a better world in our century. As August Comte said, "Ideas govern the world or throw it into chaos" and too often we have seen religion and religious ideas throwing the world into chaos instead of making the world a better place by producing better human beings.

Why do human beings need religion anyway? Is it just a crutch that people carry to avoid personal responsibility? Was the French intellectual Regis Debray accurate in saying that, "religion is no longer the opium of the people but the vitamin pill of the feeble?" Is it a tool used by the weak that holds humanity back and counters our quest for progress? Now these are all questions that I began to ask myself as I reflected on the many religious conflicts that you find all over the world. Should religion be such a key issue in the twenty-first century as stated by Tony Blair or should we aspire to create a post-religion world which will hopefully be more peaceful and united or is Albert Camus correct in saying that peace and non-violence are impossible to attain without some kind of religious belief?

America Reflects the Human Condition

A few days ago, I was up in the early hours of the morning studying for my Economics exams. Whilst delving into the theories of the likes of John Maynard Keynes and Milton Friedman, I was also listening to a popular radio station which specialises in current affairs and often has the liveliest discussions and debates on a plethora of topical issues affecting the world today.

On this morning, the topic of discussion was the death of Osama Bin Laden and whether America was justified in assassinating him in a foreign country without even having the decency to inform the host country of its intentions. Whilst many of the callers agreed that America had a right to avenge the death of so many of its citizens on September 11, 2001, many took issue with the fact that America had violated the sovereignty of another country and seemed to be unapologetic about it. For many of the callers to this radio station, this was typical American arrogance which was the reason why Americans are so loathed the world over. There was the typical round of Yankee bashing which has typified so much of the discussion amongst the thinking classes in South Africa since the USA assassinated Bin Laden in Pakistan. (Make no mistake about it, it was a planned assassination)

As I listened to the very heated exchanges I began to think about America and its role in global affairs over the last century. There are some, like Iran's late Supreme Leader Ayatollah Ruhollah Khomeini, its current Supreme Leader Ayatollah Ali Khameini and its current president Mahmoud Ahmadinejad amongst many others who believe that America is the "Great Satan" of global affairs. Others like the late American president Ronald Reagan, James Baker, George Bush Senior, George W. Bush, Barack Obama and their like would have us believe that America is the "Great Saviour" of the world.

The truth is that America is like all of us, neither completely good nor completely evil but somewhere in between. The USA, like all human beings, is capable of incredible acts of compassion and humanitarianism yet at the same time it is also capable of committing extreme acts of subterfuge, evil, and brutality. Remember that nations are made up of people, who are mostly driven by self-interest and as such nations themselves are primarily driven by self-interest in their interactions with each other. Hence it shouldn't surprise us that the USA is driven by self-interest and self-promotion in its interactions with the rest of the world. All nations are the same just as all individual human beings are the same.

It is unfair and unrealistic to expect the USA to be any different because this is contrary to our nature as human beings. Like all individual human beings, the USA is capable of acts of altruism alongside sustained acts of selfishness, self-centeredness, and self-promotion. We see the American government giving billions of dollars per annum in aid to needy countries and worthy causes, yet at the same time engaging in covert activities that destabilise certain nations and cause the deaths of so many innocent lives, all in the name of protecting and advancing US interests. We see great American entrepreneurs who have built some of the greatest corporations the world has ever seen and introduced products and services that have made life much more comfortable and pleasurable for humanity, ruthlessly advancing their business interests abroad with the help of the US government and allowing their products to be produced in countries and settings that have no respect for humane labour standards in the pursuit of profits at all costs, yet at the same time giving away billions of dollars of their own money to fight diseases and poverty in the most impoverished parts of the world.

We see the US promoting democracy in some parts of the world and doing a great service to the citizens of those affected countries by promoting openness, transparency, and freedom and yet at the same time we see the US propping up dictatorships in other parts of the world and siding with tyrants, all in the name of protecting and promoting US interests. In other words, America is a nation of many contradictions.

However, a diligent study of human nature would clearly show that all human beings share the same traits. We take a principled stand on some things and then compromise on the same issues when it suits us. We are all as individuals capable of incredible acts of goodness at times but most of our lives and our daily decisions are driven by self-interest and self-promotion. We are capable of extreme good and extreme evil at the same time as humans. This is what William Golding's epic novel; The Lord of the Flies was all about. There is good and evil within each nation, just as there is good and evil within each human being. No nation is completely good or completely evil, just as no individual human being is completely evil or completely good.

By the same token, no nation is completely altruistic or selfish, just as no individual human being is completely altruistic or selfish. With that in mind, we should not be surprised to see the contradictions and hypocrisies that often characterise the US, because an honest look at ourselves as individuals and our nations will show the same phenomenon to be inevitably true of us as well. What characterises humanity more than anything is self-contradiction, selfishness, and self-promotion and hence that is what we will see in international relations where nations interact with one another.

As we seek to construct a new world order this needs to be our starting assumption. To assume a world of nations that are driven primarily by altruism and "good" is to set ourselves up for failure. It is no secret that the nations that have been the most economically successful are the ones that have learnt to harness this desire for self-advancement and self-promotion for the greater good through the ordering and structuring of society in such a manner that this doesn't get out of hand. They haven't tried to stifle this tendency to promote self, they have just harnessed it in such a manner that whilst the self is benefitting, society as well can gain. This needs to be the kind of world order that we construct as we march forward in the 21ˢᵗ century, with hopes of a better world.

Covid-19 Crisis Calls For A Copernican Revolution

According to billionaire Johan Rupert, speaking of the Covid-19 pandemic, "people speak as if this is just a blip, but I don't think it's like anything any of us have ever seen before, economists are discussing if it's a 'V-shaped curve', or a 'U-shaped curve' — it's all meaningless. What they don't get is that this isn't just a pause — it's an entire reset of our economic system."

Rupert goes on to liken the period we have entered in the global economic system because of COVID-19 to the circumstances that the world was confronted with during the Great Depression in the 20th century.

What are we to make of this? It is clear from the words of many experts, that the world as we truly know it is over post Covid-19, and what is now to be contested is what this new global economic order will look like, as the world emerges out of this pandemic in the near future.

For us South Africans, with our plethora of socio-economic challenges, COVID-19 presents a unique opportunity to try and reset our skewed economic order so that we can exhaustively deal with those three things that are the favourite phrases of most politicians' speech writers: poverty, inequality, and unemployment.

But this will not happen through the same thinking, the same debates and the same ideological outlooks that have dominated much of our public discourse. What is needed, if we are not to waste this crisis, is a Copernican Revolution, which relates to the ground-breaking, earth-shattering discovery by Nicolaus Copernicus, that the earth was not at the centre of the universe, but rather it is the sun that is at the centre of the universe.

This Copernican Revolution, which the Italian astronomer and physicist Galileo Galilei further developed and popularised, overturned 2000 years of scientific thinking dating back to the times of the Greek philosopher Aristotle. The discovery of the simple fact that the sun, and not the earth was the gravitational centre of the universe helped spur the scientific revolution and laid a critical foundation for the later discoveries of the likes of Isaac Newton, which contributed immensely to human progress.

So, we need a similar Copernican Revolution, to reshape the world order, transform stubborn socio-economic realities that have persisted for generations and reset the global and local economic system. A Copernican Revolution of this ilk means developing and embracing completely new paradigms that are not in any way tied to what we have known up to now. It means letting go of centuries-old thinking which has been dominated by the theories of two fellows: Karl Marx and Adam Smith, and conceptualising a completely new economic and political order, not in any way influenced by the thinking of these two great thinkers. This is the challenge that is before us methinks, a Copernican Revolution that transforms the political and economic order.

In philosophy of science, a field of study which deals with metatheory, the theory behind theory, Thomas Kuhn's The Structure of Scientific Revolutions introduced the popular phrase paradigm shift to the world. Kuhn changed science, from its almost religious reliance on the scientific method, which sees scientific progress as the addition of new truths to old truths or the correction of past errors (cumulative progress building on existing ideas), to one of discontinuities.

In Kuhn's conception of scientific progress, which radically altered the field, progress consists of a series of discontinuities, where the scientific consensus of one era is challenged by outsiders from the scientific community. This plunges the scientific community into a crisis as established paradigms collapse and completely new, unrelated paradigms emerge, which is then called scientific progress.

The COVID-19 crisis allows us to move away from the same old stale debates we keep having, from outdated ideologies and outlooks, into a new economic and political era, in the mould of Kuhn's scientific progress, a Copernican Revolution built on dangerous ideas. Dangerous ideas, aptly described in the online thinktank www.edge.org are ideas to propose new ways of understanding the world and ourselves, new ways of thinking that question all our basic assumptions and new ways of ordering and structuring the world both politically and economically.

So, the opportunity beckons for us to reshape the world, and society economically and politically, through this COVID-19 crisis, in the manner that Galileo Galilei, Thomas Kuhn, and even Immanuel Kant, with his Copernican Revolution in philosophy through his iconic Critique of Pure Reason, did. It is up to us now to let go of the old and usher in the completely new.

About the author

Mugabe Ratshikuni is a writer, columnist, thought-leader, opinion-maker, scholar, entrepreneur, social activist, and civil servant. He holds a Bachelor of Arts majoring in Philosophy, Politics and Economics and a Bachelor of Arts Honours in International Politics. He is currently employed by the Gauteng Department of Human Settlements as Director: Policy and Research.

9 781067 252311